MINIMALISTIC LIVING

HOW TO LIVE IN A VAN

AND

GET OFF THE GRID

3rd Edition

by Mary Solomon

© Copyright 2014 Mary Solomon- All rights reserved.

In no way is it legal to reproduce, duplicate, or transmit any part of this document in either electronic means or in printed format. Recording of this publication is strictly prohibited and any storage of this document is not allowed unless with written permission from the publisher. All rights reserved.

The information provided herein is stated to be truthful and consistent, in that any liability, in terms of inattention or otherwise, by any usage or abuse of any policies, processes, or directions contained within is the solitary and utter responsibility of the recipient reader. Under no circumstances will any legal responsibility or blame be held against the publisher for any reparation, damages, or monetary loss due to the information herein, either directly or indirectly.

Respective authors own all copyrights not held by the publisher.

Legal Notice:

This book is copyright protected. This is only for personal use. You cannot amend, distribute, sell, use, quote or paraphrase any part or the content within this book without the consent of the author or copyright owner. Legal action will be pursued if this is breached.

Disclaimer Notice:

Please note the information contained within this document is for educational and entertainment purposes only. Every attempt has been made to provide accurate, up to date and reliable complete information. No warranties of any kind are expressed or implied. Readers acknowledge that the author is not engaging in the rendering of legal, financial or professional advice.

By reading this document, the reader agrees that under no circumstances are we responsible for any losses, direct or indirect, which are incurred as a result of the use of information contained within this document, including, but not limited to, —errors, omissions, or inaccuracies.

CONTENTS

INTRODUCTION

MINIMALISM 101

THE BENEFITS OF LIVING WITH LESS

BABY STEPS: STARTING YOUR MINIMALIST JOURNEY

MINIMALISTIC CONCERNS

HARDCORE MINIMALISM: GOING OFF THE GRID

OFF THE GRID LIVING IN A VAN

FINDING THE RIGHT VEHICLE

OTHER CONSIDERATIONS WHEN BUYING YOUR LIVING VAN

CHECKING OUT THE VAN BEFORE BUYING

ACCESSORIZING

SAFETY

TESTING YOUR MOBILE HOME

SELECTING YOUR DESTINATION

SUPPLIES NEEDED

WHERE TO GO

<u>IN CASE OF EMERGENCIES</u>

<u>SUCCESS STORIES: LIVING IN A VAN</u>

<u>CONCLUSION</u>

Introduction

Living in a car or van can be a great way to spend the summer or step off the grid! It sounds like the start of a good movie! Adventure is something most of us could use more of in our lives. Living in a car or van can be a way to do something new, refreshing, and exciting.

Many people are doing all they can to cut costs. In many situations, living in a vehicle is less expensive than a house payment or apartment rental. Car camping, as some call it, can help reduce stress on the budget and also make it possible to enjoy the simple things in life.

Living in a car or van is a great way for a couple to learn more about each other! No more distractions of a normal home living relationship. What a great way to get to know each other! For long term relationships, living in a van can be a way to move into a deeper understanding of one another, and enrich the relationship.

Save money, get out of debt, travel, and step off the grid all at the same time!

This book will help you come up with creative, safe, resourceful ideas to help ensure that you have an enjoyable journey.

Minimalism 101

"A well-used minimum suffices for everything." – Jules Verne, Around The World In 80 Days

For most of us, it seems that having more stuff makes for greater living sufficiency and on the flip side, having less equals scarcity and inability to meet needs. But Jules Verne made a very interesting point about the relationship of met needs, personal satisfaction and the amount of stuff we have. In fact, his statement is what minimalism is about.

Minimalism is a way of living that gets rid of unnecessary or unused things that lead to a simple and uncluttered life. It's a living a life free from being addicted to things and accumulating them and being able to freely enjoy life especially those things that are truly important and that can give lasting contentment and joy.

Minimalism may be considered a way out of the many, many excesses this world has thrown our way, which includes materialism, clutter, consumerism, excess debt, too many things to do, excess noise and distractions. And unfortunately, these things have very little meaning in our lives, if any.

Minimalism often brings to mind things like throwing everything – or at least most things – away, how immoral buying new stuff is or living in a small, cramped prison cell-like room with nothing inside. Honestly, it can be like that when taken to the extreme. The good news about minimalism is that often times, it isn't like that.

While it's true that minimalism does entail getting rid of lots of stuff, it's actually just a result of minimalism. You may be a philanthropist and give tons of stuff away to lots of people but that doesn't make you anywhere near being a minimalist. Heck, Bill Gates gives away more stuff (or money) than the Red Cross or other huge charitable institutions but he is by no means a minimalist. However important a part giving away lots of things is in living a minimalist lifestyle, it's just a part and isn't really needed if it's not in line with your priorities.

Speaking of priorities, it's what being a minimalist is really about. If you know your priorities, you can throw or give away everything else that isn't in line with them. Think of minimalism in the same vein as ultra marathon running. Those ultra marathoners have very little body fat and wear the lightest and only the most necessary of clothing – stripping off anything that may be considered excess be it body fat or clothes – in order to run as light and unimpeded as possible. When you consider that the minimum distance for an ultra marathon is 50 kilometers, you'll see why it's important for them to ditch anything unnecessary.

Minimalism means being able to say with conviction and an unbreakable certainty that this or that is important in our lives. I, for example, value my relationship with my wife, whose love language is quality time. Knowing that, I try to keep my schedule as free as possible to be able to spend as much time as I can with her. I don't entertain regular nights out for a run or bike ride (occasional ones are ok) because I know that one of my priorities is my marriage.

For other people, the most important thing for them is to be able to give to their church or help the poor and needy by giving them stuff. As such, they realize they don't need a lot of things to survive and are able to save money to be able to do what's most important for them like giving regularly to their churches or giving stuff to the poor and needy.

If you're considering giving a minimalist lifestyle a try, take baby steps first. You don't need to give all your stuff away like Saint Francis – he even gave away the clothes he's wearing and simply retained his birthday suit. You can start by taking the time to really think about what's really important to you. Only then will you know if you're already living a minimalist lifestyle or if you're living with too much excess that can even add stress to your life.

If after taking the time to think about what's important, you realized you want to live with much less stuff, you'll need to take an inventory of the stuff that you currently have. You won't know how much to get rid off if in the first place, you don't know how much and what you currently have. Right? Right!

Your ability to live a meaningful, rich and beautiful life isn't dependent on how much stuff you have because most of the best things in life – those that give us much joy and fulfillment – aren't material. Those things include deep and meaningful relationships, being able to live out one's life purpose or mission, and being able to make a huge difference in the lives of others. It's important to keep in mind however, that the amount of stuff needed for living such a life is totally arbitrary, i.e., different for everyone. As such, you shouldn't compare yourself and what you believe to be your level of material needs to others.

Another thing to note about minimalism is that you should avoid getting rid of things that are important or meaningful for you. Again, consider the core of minimalism is priorities. If you get rid of things that are important to you or are needed for your priorities, that's not minimalism. That's ascetism. And that will just make you feel sad and even more unfulfilled, which can lead you to buy more of the same stuff that you just got rid off. Take baby steps and test out the waters before you go minimalist.

The Benefits Of Living With Less

One of the best things about being a minimalist is that you free up a lot of resources that can be redirected to those areas of your life that are truly important to you, which minimizes wastage. For example, I don't mind buying a brand new Macbook Pro laptop that's more expensive than most other brands because apart from it being one of the most efficient and durable laptops around, I have the money to buy it because I don't indulge in many other things like expensive clothes or annual out-of-the-country trips like most of my other friends do. Besides, the Macbook Pro laptop is an important part of my life because I used it for my work. I'd rather buy it at a premium of twice the price of a budget laptop that I'll need to replace in a 2 years because Macbooks are known to last forever. Alright, that's an exaggeration but 5-7 years isn't unheard of for the brand.

Always keep in mind that minimalism isn't a religion that's legalistic with so many dos and don'ts. It's a guide to living – a set of practices if you will – that can help you get the most joy and meaning out of life. And although it isn't a strict set of rules and regulations, adhering to many of its practices leads to many benefits such as:

-Personal Significance And Contentment: Living with less stuff can help you wean yourself off your dependence or obsessions with material things and in the process, help you experience the true and lasting joys of contentment and a sense of personal significance. Many people go bankrupt with mountains of credit card bills because of buying too much stuff they can't even afford to buy in the first place, thinking that the more they have, the more content they'll be. They also tie the amount of stuff owned to their self-worth, which aggravates the situation even more. Materialism is flame and buying more stuff to feel content is like pouring gasoline on it.

On the other hand, starving the materialism beast by getting rid of stuff you don't need or aren't related to your priorities weaken it and eventually, maim it fatally. Contentment and a sense of significance are often interconnected so when you become more content in life, you experience a greater sense of personal significance and vice versa. Minimalism helps you experience both by starving and killing the materialism beast.

-Freedom: Believe it or not, clutter has a way of keeping us from moving on from our pasts, especially undesirable ones. This is because clutter or stuff has a tendency to remind us of past events and reminisce. Another way of looking at it is this: the more space your past takes up, the less you have for new ones. Minimalism helps you get rid of clutter and help you free up more space for new and better experiences. You enjoy the freedom of moving forward unhindered by past events.

-Less Is More: Minimalism (less) allows you to enjoy better things in life (more quality). When you go minimal, you'll be surprised at the amount of money you can get to save – money that you can redirect to things that have a greater ability to make your life more meaningful and joyful. For me, that included my Macbook Pro that I use to earn a living. Using such a great laptop makes me even more productive and I was only able to afford it because I didn't frivolously spend my money on things that are inferior in life quality, i.e., those that aren't really that important to me like frequent out-of-the-country travels and expensive clothing.

As I mentioned earlier, minimalism is arbitrary, and the same goes with what you'll consider to be of higher life quality to you. What's important to you may not be to others and vice versa. But the point being is that minimalism can help you live a much fuller and more meaningful life.

-Practicality: One of minimalism's most obvious benefits is spending less. Because you need fewer things, you need less money. If you're able to maintain your earning power, then you can actually get to save money and become even more financially independent. Contrary to most people's belief that more money is the only key to financial independence, frugality or practicality is the other half – it may even be the more important one. When you look at celebrities that have gone bankrupt, it's clear that more money isn't necessarily the answer to financial independence.

-Less Maintenance: When I had one car, the maintenance was manageable both financially and in terms of maintenance work to be done. After getting married and having a second car (the other one is for my wife), maintenance became a burden. Not only do I have to pay for regular maintenance of 2 cars, I also have to clean, monitor and take care of 2. I don't know about you but to me, it's a burden.

When you have so many furniture and appliances at home, you have more spaces for dust and grime to accumulate, which will require more tedious cleaning. Compare it to a living room with just a table, sofa set and a T.V. – it's very easy to clean compared to one with vases, cabinets that contain stuff you don't use and other ornaments like lamps stands and unused tables and chairs. Minimalist living relieves you of much work required to maintain a clean living space.

-It's Harder To Lose Things: When you live in a clutter-free or minimalist home, you not only have less things to lose but you also have less places to lose your stuff in. You don't have a lot of nooks and crannies to lose your car keys or cellular phones in. You have fewer obstacles to storing and finding things easier.

Baby Steps: Starting Your Minimalist Journey

"Anything you dream [can] be yours simply because you've focused on the steps you could take instead of the distance to get there." – A.J. Darkholme, Rise Of The Morningstar

As a famous Chinese saying goes, the journey of a thousand miles starts with one step. The minimalist lifestyle isn't a trivial lifestyle choice that you can just instantly switch on to. It's radical lifestyle change that will really change your, well, life! And for such changes to last long and result in meaningful changes, you'll have to take your time and start with baby steps. And speaking of baby steps, here are some ways you can first frolic in the minimalism waters before diving into the deep. Doing so can help you transition into it much better and keep you from being overwhelmed with lifestyle changes and increase your chances of successfully going minimalist.

Clothing

It seems that the Pareto Principle isn't just applicable to personal productivity. It's also applicable to our personal fashion! Some statistics estimate that most people wear only 20% of their whole wardrobe 80% of the time. What this implies is that yes, there is much room for minimizing. There's on average, about 80% of our wardrobe that may no longer be relevant or important to us and are simply taking up valuable space.

To start frolicking in the minimalist waters, begin by taking an inventory of your current wardrobe and honestly assess which clothes are no longer important or relevant to your. Get rid of those either by taking the higher road of donating to charity (institutions or friends) or holding a garage sale (more money). Not only is it possible for you to have extra cash, you also get to have more free space! Talk about a win-win situation, eh?

Home Furniture

If your muscles are up for the challenge, this is one of the best ways to free up a lot of physical and mental space in your life. Not only can it give you more space to more around, it will also reduce the amount of time and effort needed to clean your home – less stuff requires less cleaning. It also improves your abode's lighting and airflow. If you're iffy about permanently getting rid of furniture, you can consider doing a trial run and find a temporary place to store excess furniture.

House Decors

Believe or not, house decors are one of the most space-consuming and cluttering items in your home, especially if many of these hold no real or sentimental value to us. Most of the time, they're simply there because they match the overall color scheme of our home or room or because we're raised up to be uncomfortable with unfilled spaces at home. These things tend to be distractive and can also require a great deal of time and effort to maintain, e.g., clean.

Start running through your home with a very keen eye on decors that don't serve a good purpose and that are simply there to either fill up space or to decorate for the sake of doing so. You may be pleasantly surprised to find just how much clutter you can remove and space you can free up. You may also be pleasantly surprised to earn some money if you hold a garage sale for those decors.

Television Sets

According to a survey conducted by Nielsen many years ago, Americans on average watch about 4.5 hours of TV daily and – check this out – there are more TV sets than people in the average American household. Moreover, the survey revealed that TV sets are turned on for an average of 8 hours daily in the average American household.

If you think it's excessive...well it really is. And if you consider that TV-watching is as productive as counting the blades of grass in a football field, you'll realize that spending too much time on the boob tube is literally a great waste of time.

Consider reducing both the number of TV sets at home and the amount of viewing time. Watch only the shows that you're really interested in or are important. Not only will you free up space, you'll also free up time for more meaningful activities – like family time – and save on electricity. You might end up with some cash too if you sell the unnecessary TVs.

Counters

One of the most cluttered – and distracting – places at home are the counters or counter-tops. When there are too many things on the counter-tops, workable spaces tend to be limited and can distract you from doing what you need to do quickly and efficiently. For most people, which may or may not include you, too many items that clutter counter-tops have been there for so long that they're hardly noticed as clutter or distractions despite being such. Once they're removed however, the marked difference is easily noticeable.

As a good baby step towards going minimalist, try this for at least 7 days: Remove your counter-tops' clutter even if you honestly believe you need them there and keep them in boxes or drawers – anywhere where they won't be seen but can still be accessed easily. If you really believe these are relevant and important, return them to their former places. If not, keep them hidden and stored. Chances are you'll keep them hidden and stored because of the marked difference you'll see in 7 days.

Cooking Ware And Utensils

I've never seen a kitchen – however big – that has enough space for cooking ware and utensils. And if you consider the fact that our grandparents and great grandparents were able to consistently come up with richly delicious culinary feasts in much smaller kitchens, you'll realize that most kitchens – probably including yours – are overstuffed with too many unnecessary and irrelevant things. You'll also realize that often times, delicious foods are those that are simplest to cook.

That being said, it's almost certain to say that you have way too much cookware and utensils in your kitchen that takes up too much space. To start frolicking in the minimalist waters, try storing away all the non-basic cooking ware and kitchen utensils in boxes or drawers. And just as with house decors, return them after 7 days if you see that those really needed to be where they were. Chances are, you'll keep them stored and hidden too.

Toys

Having too many toys can spoil your children, not to mention keep them from the more important things like studying well, developing a sense of contentment and delayed gratification among others. If your kids are already grown up, keeping those toys around eats up space and is a great source of clutter. Fewer toys then, mean less clutter. It also means that your kids have more opportunities to develop good character and study well for school, which are what's really more important for your children's personal growth and future success.

Minimalistic Concerns

One of the concerns about minimalistic living is that it's one that's boring, empty, sparse or all of it. It's normally thought of as living like a hermit in the boondocks or out in the wild away from any possible signs of human life. As much as I'd like to refute that claim, I can't. It's because minimalism can be like that – but only if taken to the extreme. But a minimalist life that works is one that's centered on stripping away only those that aren't really necessary for you personally. If some people can live like hermits and find joy in it, then that kind of minimalist living is one that works – for them. Again, you don't need to ditch your smart phone to live a minimalist life. What you'll need to ditch are those that aren't in line with your life's most important priorities in order to make more room for those that are.

Others believe that being minimalist extends to daily eating in that you have to be a vegetarian or a vegan. Yes, you can simplify your diet to a vegan or vegetarian one – a very healthy diet by the way – but again, it doesn't have to be that way. Yes, if your priority is health, the environment and ethical treatment of animals, then going vegan or vegetarian is obviously a great way to go minimalist. But if your definition of PETA is People Eating Tasty Animals, then going minimalist doesn't have to include going vegetarian or vegan.

Believe it or not, a daily schedule is also one aspect many people think are a requirement for living a minimalist lifestyle. In particular, some believe that you're supposed to impose a limit or cap as to the number of activities that should be done everyday and that exceeding such a limit is akin to ditching the minimalist lifestyle. As with food, the items on your schedule are important to a minimalist lifestyle only to the extent of their importance or relevance to your life priorities. The only activities you'll need to limit, or even eliminate, are those that keep you from truly focusing and enjoying your life priorities. It just so happens that often times, stripping off unnecessary or irrelevant activities lead to a whole lot more free time.

Legalism is another concern about minimalism. Maybe it's because many "lifestyles" like diets and religion have imposed very strict rules and regulations on their practitioners that the same impressions have been imposed on minimalism. Truth is, minimalism has no set of rules and that there's no single way of living a minimalist lifestyle. Yes, there are many suggestions on how to do it but that's what they are – merely suggestions. They're not rules. The only rule, if you may call it that, when it comes to minimalism is stripping away as much unrelated and irrelevant stuff as possible in your life. Even that is totally up to you. You determine what is truly important and relevant to your life priorities and even then, if you'd get rid of them or not and to what extent. You determine what the minimum is for your life, not others.

Frugality is an aspect of minimalism that's very much misunderstood. First, the impression is that being frugal means settling for the cheapest possible alternative there is. Although there are times that doing so is the most frugal thing to do, it isn't like that always. You can still be frugal even if you buy the most expensive brand. Why? Because frugality is about sticking to the essentials, what's really important in terms of your life's priorities. Going back to my Macbook experience, buying the thing was the frugal thing to do because of its very high quality and durability. As I mentioned earlier, buying the cheapest laptop that will work optimally for about 2 years tops will cost me more in 6 to 7 years because Macbooks are known to work well for a long time, which I take to believe as 5 to 7 years. How do I know? My mother in law's Macbook White – an earlier and lower model – is still working well after 6 years! The only thing she needed to change on the 5th year was the battery! You can be frugal and still enjoy nice things in life every now and then, particularly if it's a need.

Lastly, many people are concerned that living a minimalist lifestyle means commuting for the rest of your life, i.e., you can't drive your own car. Again, it may be the case only if it's in line with your life priorities and you don't have to commute all the days of your life if it isn't important or relevant to your life's priorities. In fact, one of the most hardcore ways of living a minimalist lifestyle would need a private vehicle: a van!

Hard Core Minimalism: Going Off The Grid

"I've lived a slower and less expensive life going off the grid, and I'm happier because of it." – Ed Begley, Jr., American actor and environmentalist

Billions of people all around the world check out their mailboxes at similar times of the month expecting to find the usual mailbox fillers – water, power, telephone and other utility bills. With the continuing rise in the financial and environmental cost of these utilities, more and more people are desperately looking for ways to reduce, minimize or even detach from these utility services by going off the grid.

Going off the grid has become – and continues to become – increasingly popular these days. From simply cutting down on expenses to joining the ranks of Captain Planet's vast army of environmental protectors, going off the grid has become the lifestyle of choice for many people – and they don't regret the choice. But what does going "off-grid" mean exactly?

Grid is associated with electricity – power grids – and the interconnected systems that deliver it to households. Normally, a house is hooked up to a power line to be able to enjoy electricity, which is practically impossible to live without these days. Over time, the term grid has come to be associated with being linked to a utility system that includes gas, water and telephone.

Going off the grid means to detach one's self or household from the networks of utility companies and live independently of them. Going off the grid doesn't necessarily mean living a primitive life and shunning all utility systems. Yes, many people have done that but you can also do it partially. You can disconnect from some while keeping connected to others. I think in this day and age, you can't totally go off the grid unless you're ready to be a hermit so even partially going off the grid can be a major accomplishment already.

Although getting accurate figures as to the exact number of Americans living off the grid, an estimate is available. Home Power magazine estimated that in 2006, about 180,000 homes were already able to generate their own electricity and were no longer dependent on the electricity companies. The popular publication USA Today also estimated that about 27,000 houses used wind and solar energy for their needs in an article published in April 2006. I suspect that more people have gone off-grid since then. And if you find yourself wanting to embrace a more minimalist lifestyle after taking the baby steps, then going off the grid may just be the thing for you too.

There are important areas you'll need to address if you want to go off-grid, partial or otherwise. These are electricity, water, toilet and cooking.

Electricity

When we talk about electricity for powering the home, there are 2 kinds: DC (Direct Current) and AC (Alternating

Current). Devices that run on DC electricity include lights, ventilation fans, water pumps and others that you can safely plug into a socket of 12 volts. Devices that run on AC include microwave ovens and air conditioners as well as devices that you can plug in 120-volt outlets.

When living off-grid, there are 3 ways to generate electricity: solar, wind and hydro. The most popular among the 3 is solar power, which makes use of photovoltaic solar panels (solar panels for brevity), an electric inverter and batteries. The solar panels catch the sun's rays and turn them into electricity. The electric inverter converts the electricity generated by the solar panels (DC or Direct Current) into AC (Alternating Current), which is what home appliances like computers, air conditioners, refrigerators and TV sets run on. Most appliances, especially those that aren't rechargeable, are made to run on AC electricity because the power grids were made to run on such owing to its ability to be transmitted over long distances, e.g. from the power plants to homes and offices. Finally, the batteries are needed to store electricity produced during the day for use in the evening, when the solar panels are at their utmost uselessness.

Solar panels can generate provide a lot of electricity for a really long time, especially in the sunniest areas of the world. Since it also doesn't have any moving parts, it only requires very little maintenance. After installing it, you can practically forget about it and it'll do its job faithfully and consistently. Well, as consistent as the sun showing itself at least.

The current downside to solar panels is the steep price powering an entire home exclusively with solar power. This concern may be addressed over the long term as more and more people use solar panels and make mass-production economical and profitable. The other concern, however, is something that's completely out of our hands: variances in solar exposure, i.e., the amount of time and the intensity of daily sunlight. It'll be practically impossible to generate power on stormy or cloudy days.

The second way of generating off-grid electricity is by harnessing the power of the wind via residential wind turbines. Compared to solar power however, this is way less dependable for sustained electricity because average wind speed is way more volatile than sunlight. As such, this takes more effort on your part in terms of having to monitor and estimate average wind speeds to determine how much electricity you can generate for your home.

When using wind turbines, their sizes really do matter. If you plan to power a few appliances only, a wind turbine with a diameter of 4 feet can produce 400 watts and should be enough. If you plan to consistently power most or all appliances in your home, you'll have to generate about 10,000 watts of electricity using a wind turbine with a diameter of about 23 feet, which you'll have to mount on a 100-foot tower.

The 3rd way of generating your own electricity is through a micro-hydro system. Simply put, this is a retail-sized version of those big hydroelectric power plants that supply a big chunk of electricity to power grids all over the country. As with the industrial counterparts, this system uses a running source of water such as a river or stream. Water running from a higher plane to a lower one turns an electricity-generating turbine, which is located near or at the bottom end of the stream or river.

Using a micro-hydro system may just be the best among the 3 because of its cost efficiency, says Energy Alternatives Ltd., a leading Canadian alternative energy company. According to them, electricity produced by such a system can be up to

100 times more than solar panels or wind turbines for the same cost or investment because if you have a good source of naturally running water, it will run your turbines for about, well, all the time! Unless off course there's a very severe drought that sucks the running source of water dry. But then again, that's highly improbable.

The only possible drawback? It's also site-specific, meaning you'll need to have a good source of naturally running water near your home. Otherwise, you can't use this system.

Water

One of the best ways I know to go off the grid in terms of a water system is having a portable system and for this, you'll need to invest in a device called RinseKit, which is a pressurized tank of water that includes a hose that you can hide inside and is portable, weighing just 24 pounds when filled with water. It looks pretty much like your regular toolbox in that it opens and closes like it. The RinseKit, which was invented by surfer dude Chris Crawford, is very popular among surfers, campers and pretty much everyone who likes going off the grid and needs a good source of water for washing stuff and taking a bath.

The RinseKit retails for about $90 on Amazon.com and can store up to 2 gallons of water that can be "showered" or spurted out for several minutes, depending on the strength setting. For example, the 2-gallon reservoir can sprayed continuously for up to 3 minutes before running out if set on shower mode.

You can re-fill the thing at home or wherever you can get tap water. It's also environmentally friendly since it doesn't use electricity and it's friendly to you body too because it doesn't have to be pumped – the pressure is provided by your tap water source. The kit's box chamber can hold up to 65 psi of pressure to help ensure a good water spray for you.

Waste Management

No, I'm not talking of trash and garbage alone. I'm talking about your personal waste, if you know what I mean. It's alright, no need to be ashamed talking about it. The thing with most of us "civilized" and "cultured" people is that we're no longer talking about our personal waste management, like it's such a big taboo of ancient proportions. This is the case because we live in a very sanitized society wherein we're bred to be totally dependent on the grid to live, which includes the sewerage system. But living off-grid will require you to go back to managing your own personal waste because if you don't, you'll – pardon the pun – stink.

So how do you handle or manage your personal waste? First, let's look at the 2 different waste products our bodies produce: urine (wiwi) and bowel (poopee). It's much easier to handle wiwi, especially for men – and I don't mean that in a chauvinistic way. You can practically pee anywhere when you're out in nature – behind a bush, tree or on an open piece of soil. Just be careful to avoid peeing near camps (yours or others'), rivers, lakes and other natural bodies of water. It's also best to avoid peeing at the same place all the time to minimize or prevent odor build up. Of course, if you're near a public restroom, that'd be great.

When you're in a tight spot without the benefit of nature or a public restroom, you can use a yellow-colored Nalgene kind of bottle, which can be very discrete for peeing. Aside from such bottles' abilities to seal liquids in very well, the yellow color won't make it obvious to others that you're actually carrying pee. Just empty out the contents when you get to a restroom or an open lot of nature and you're good to go. For women, there's a neat product called Go Girl, which is a female urination device (FUD) that allows women to pee like a man, i.e., standing up, in a tube whenever, wherever. That's a great equalizing device, if you ask me.

While peeing may be relatively easy to manage, it's not the same for defecating or pooping, especially for people who live in a van. So how do you do it off the grid? The easiest way is to use what are called cat holes, which you can easily make in a vacant lot of soil. Simply dig a cat hole that's at least 12 inches deep, poop in it and cover it up again with soil. If you don't, you run the risk of wild animals that have a poopee fetish digging it up again. Also, make sure your cat hole is at least 151 feet away from any naturally occurring body of water such as lakes, rivers and streams. The drawback to this is that it's very uncomfortable because, let's face it, digging holes and covering them everytime can be tiring. Oh, and there's the issue of privacy and comfort, of course.

I highly advise using a toilet cabana when peeing or pooping in public or open land. A toilet cabana is simply a tent that looks like an outhouse, which can give you a great sense of privacy for a smoother and easier peeing or pooping time. You can also shower in it using your RinseKit.

Another way of defecating off the grid is by using 5-gallon buckets lined with at least 2 trash bags for pooping. After pooping in it, simply tie the bags up to seal and throw in the trash. It's no different from throwing baby and animal diapers with baby and animal poopees in them but why do people find it gross if it's filled adult poopee? Is it because babies and animals are cuter than most adults? Come to think of it, poopee is poopee, regardless of the cuteness (or lack thereof) of the source. If you find the rim of the bucket to be uncomfortable on your buttocks, you can line it with a piece of pipe insulation and duct tape it so it'll hold. If you have more budget, you can also buy a portable toilet seat that you can simply snap on the 5-gallon bucket such as the Luggable Loo toilet seat to make your defecating experience a comfortable one.

A good alternative to the 1st two methods is the Porta-Potti, which as the name implies, is a portable toilet system that can hold several servings of poopies and wiwies. The stored "inventory" can be unloaded either at an RV dump station or at a public toilet – take your pick! Most people are able to for as much as 2 weeks before having to unload the inventory but I highly suggest that the longest you go prior to dumping the goods at your friendly neighborhood RV dump station or public toilet is just 1 week. Can you imagine the stench of 2 weeks' worth of inventory? Ewweee!!!

The Porta-Potties come in 2 parts: the fresh water holder and the fecal inventory holder. After every "session", you flush it with the stored fresh water that runs on the sides to clean the toilet. I highly suggest you use a deodorizing agent to help minimize the odor and – as hip-hoppers would always say – break it down! The fecal inventory holder does a really good sealing job that you shouldn't be smelling any of the inventory prior to opening and unloading. You simply detach the fecal holder to unload.

Cooking

When talking about cooking off the grid, most people would conjure visions of campfires or something like it. Sure, that's one way of cooking food sans the utility companies and comforts of a regular on-the-grid kitchen but there are other ways of doing it. One of them is the Crisis Cooker.

The Crisis Cooker is a one that can use fuel, wood and charcoal to cook food – boil, fry or grill them all. With such versatility in terms of fuel source and cooking functions, it has become one of the favorite cooking systems for many people who are off the grid. On average, the Crisis Cooker uses about 6 briquettes of charcoal to cook a meal and can be used after just 10 minutes of preheating. The whole thing weights around 25 lbs. and can go for up to 3 weeks of cooking 2 meals daily with a 25 pounds of charcoal.

Another alternative cooking system for going off-grid are rocket stoves that are well known due to their ability to quickly heat things up. Most of these babies are homemade and can set you back an average of $100. Unlike the Crisis Cooker however, rocket stoves only use dry leaves, small twigs and other small flammable materials to create a sustainable fire. A testament to its heating efficiency: it can generate enough heat to quickly boil a pot of water using just 5 pieces of common twigs. For a homemade but non-portable variant, you can use common bricks to make your own.

Aside from the 2 aforementioned cooking systems, another alternative for off-grid cooking needs is a rocket mass heater, which is like a rocket stove but much bigger. This stove uses wood for fuel and can also function as a masonry heater or heating system. Normally, wood is fed into a combustion chamber and the generated heat pushes the gases into another but insulated combustion chamber. This type of cooking/heating system's downside is that it isn't portable so if you're looking to live in a van, forget about this.

Barrel stoves are a portable cooking alternative that can be used to both warm food and purify water. For people who love to do things themselves (DIY), barrel stoves are something that can be done at home using a 55-gallon steel drum, regular tools, hinges, screws, carriage bolts and L-brackets.

For sterilizing drinking water or simply to make hot coffee or tea, one good investment for off-grid living is the Hot Water Rocket. This device can give you hot water quickly and weighs a mere 2 pounds and stands no more than 2 feet tall, which makes it a very portable water heating system ideal for off-grid living. Oh, and did I mention it's solar powered? Cool, huh?

Off The Grid Living In A Van

Why on earth would somebody want to live in a van instead of a house? I know, it sounds kind of weird to think that somebody would, right? But truth is, lots of people do want to live in a van…and many actually do. Clearly, there are very good reasons why they live in their vans, though it may not seem to be very obvious at first glance.

So really, why would people want to live in a van? Why should you? Why don't we check out one of the most popular "vandwellers" in America, Ken Ilgunas, who also authored the book on his vandwelling experience Walden On Wheels: On The Open Road From Debt To Freedom. He wrote in his article for the Huffington Post the following reasons for living in a van:

A Simple Life

Life couldn't be any simpler than living in a van. Apart from buying a good second-hand van and the basic living equipment, you don't need anything else. You'll really get to live life as close to the basics as possible. You won't have to worry about doing so many things just to maintain your abode. A simple life can be one of great joy because many of the best things in life aren't just free, they're also simple.

It's Cheap

The usual partner of simple living is cheap living. Consider the expense comparison made by Ken Ilgunas: Average apartment and dormitory rentals are $1,000 and $800 monthly, respectively, compared to his total cost of $1,500 for the van and average weekly living expenses of only $103. Now, do the math. You can save a lot of money for those things that are really important for you, which is the goal of minimalism, remember?

The cost of housing has reached really high proportions. It is almost impossible to find a place that is livable and comfortable that is not going to take up the majority of your income and then you have to try to make the rest of it stretch enough in order to get you through the rest of the month in food, gas, clothing, and all of the other things that you need or you need to find a second job. It can get frustrating to think that so much of your money is going to rent that is supporting another person rather than being spent on things that you would like. This is one of the first things that people will think about when they are looking into living in a van. They think about how much cheaper it would be to live in their own space, not give money to another person who never helps them out when something is going wrong at the dwelling, and to save money to use for other things.

Housing costs are one thing that is going to take up a huge portion of your budget. If you live in one of the more expensive areas of the country you might spend over half of your budget just to pay off the rent each month. This might not be as high in other parts of the country, but no matter where you are living you will end up spending a huge part of your income on a property that does not belong to you and which is just lining the pockets of someone else and making them rich. If you are able to get rid of those housing costs simply by living in a van, you will be able to get that much of your income back each month and can use it for savings, paying off your debts and your student loans, and anything else that you might need to survive.

Even in the cities you are going to be able to find places that you can park the van that is going to save you even more money in the long run. Even if you do end up needing to rent a place to keep your van, for safety reasons or to make sure you are in the right parking spot and do not get towed or in trouble, the rent on most parking spots is going to be less than $100 a month in most parts of the country. This is way less than the 50% of your income that most of your apartments are going to cost and this can help you with your budget over time.

Think about all of the things that you can do with that money once you are able to use it for other things rather than your rent. You can spend it on things like eating better, going on vacation, paying off your student loans, paying off other debts that you have, and even saving up for your future such as your 401k or a new house. There is so much that you are going to be able to do with this extra money just by living in a van.

Oh, you don't just get to save on rent and other living expenses, you also get to save on tax expenses. Even if you live in a traditional home and are not renting, you can find that there are some benefits in living out of your van. When you are living in a traditional home, you will find that the property taxes can get really expensive. You might find that living out of a van and selling your home can save you a lot of money in the long run and you can use it on other things rather than having to give that money in to the government each month. Even if you do want to own a home, living out of a van can help you to save a lot of money.

Those who choose to live in a big city will find that the property taxes are a whole lot higher than living out in the country, but the commute can kill them as well. Instead of having to worry about this, you could purchase a home in the country that has lower property taxes and then live out of your van during the week. You can then get the lower property taxes while saving on the commute at the same time.

This can also be a way to save you money so that you are able to purchase a home. You could stop paying rent for a couple of years and instead of giving that money to a landlord who is just sitting and doing nothing all day, you can put it aside to use towards a new house. This will make the process a lot easier because you are able to put more and more money towards the home and can move in a lot faster.

Celibacy

Depending on who's talking, this can be an advantage for vandwellers. Why? Would you actually consider making love in a van where it isn't only very tight but also run the risk of being accosted by the traffic authorities. For people who value their spirituality, this means being able to live a holier than usual life and the opportunity to focus on higher-order priorities like, well, travel.

It Can Actually Be Comfortable

Contrary to public perception, living inside a van can be comfortable. The negative opinion seems to stem from the fact that people just think of stock vans, i.e., vans that are the same as when they first came out of the showroom and weren't modified for living in. With some ingenuity and creativity, you can customize your van to be a beautiful and comfortable abode, which is pretty cheap to maintain too.

More Control Over Your Life

Ken quoted another famous vandweller, Bob Wells, as saying: "You have so small a space you have to get rid of everything. If you buy something, there's no room left. So something has to go." This kind of living arrangement keeps you from hoarding stuff, which is a sign that you're not in control of your life, particularly materialism. You learn to buy and keep only what's necessary, which helps starve the beast of materialism to death and strengthen your control over your life.

More Intimacy With Nature

When you live in a van, there's less buffer against the outside world, hence giving you a greater sense of connection with Mother Nature, especially if you decide to park and live in a place with less man-made structures. When it rains, you hear the pitter-patter of the rain over your van's roof louder than you ever would inside a house, which makes you "feel" nature even better. You can also park for as long as you want in a place where there are lots of trees or rich foliage to enjoy Mother Nature until you feel one with her. You can't feel her in such ways when you simply live in a modern home, especially in an urban area.

Live In Different Places And Experience Different Cultures (Cultural Crusader)

Vandwelling is mobile living. While some people spend so much on living expenses on top of travel ones just to enjoy different cultures. Living in a van gives you the opportunity to live in many different places at a much lower cost because you don't need to stay in a hotel or rent an apartment in order to live in many places you'd like to visit, especially if they're reachable by land travel. With the opportunity to stay in a particular place longer, you get the chance to experience that particular place's culture on a deeper level. You don't just get to be a tourist – you also get to be a resident even for just a while.

What is the one thing that most people say they would like to do when they retire? Most people will say that they would like to travel the world and see a lot of the things that they have never had time to see when they were growing up and raising kids and all of the other big things that kept them busy through life. But why do you need to wait until you are getting decrepit and old in order to travel? You might not be in the condition to do the traveling that you had dreamt of for so long because you are too tired or you have a health concern that is stopping you. If you live out of a van now, you will be able to travel at any time that you want. You will be able to park your van in almost any location that you want. If you are traveling and decide that you like a place, you can just stop there and enjoy it for as long as you like. If you ever get tired of this place, you just have to put your stuff back in the van and then go to where you would like. You can follow anything that you like whether it is your whims, a band that you love, and the seasons. It is all up to you and you do not have to worry about anything bothering you or to get old to do it.

Take Part In A Cultural Heritage Of Vagabonding

Particularly in the United States, people have a long-standing history and heritage of living on the road. From the Western days of the Conestoga wagons to the Volkswagen riding hippies of the 70's, it's clear that living on the road –

and consequently in vehicles – are part of a rich cultural heritage.

Drawing The Line Between Needs And Wants

Living in a van is as minimalist as it comes. This kind of lifestyle draws a very clear line between needs and wants, which in today's society seems to be a very, very vague one. Consider the average teenager today on leaving their cellular phones at home, losing them or not having one: "I need my phone! I'm gonna die without it!" Really? It seems that many kids today – even adults – have become technovores too. But when you live a life that's as simple as one in a van, you'll have the opportunity to really see and know what real needs are, not what mass marketing hucksters brainwash you with.

Freedom!

No doubt about it, a minimalist life in a van can offer you much freedom that even all the money in the world couldn't. Especially if you do freelance work over the Internet, you can go wherever you want, wake up whenever you want and work at your particular time of choice during the day. Now if that's not freedom, I don't know what is!

Other Good Reasons

There are probably times in your life when you have thought about the future and thought how if you had enough money you would go and do one thing or another. It seems like everyone has these kinds of dreams but there are some things that are always going to be in the way. Often the thing that is going to be getting in your way is the fact that you do not have enough money in order to follow the dream.

If you are paying for your rent, utility bills, furniture, food, and all of your other bills, it can be really difficult to save up any extra money at the end of the month in order to see that dream become a reality. This issue can be fixed simply by living out of your van. You will no longer have to pay for rent that is going to save you a ton of money. You will also be able to save money on furniture and utility bills that is going to save you even more.

It is easy to see that you are able to save a ton of money if you are able to get rid of these big expenses from your life and you will be able to use that money in any other way that you choose. The money that you might have spent on a car payment or a house can then be used on making your dreams and thoughts turn into a reality. Just make sure to spend the money in a wise way and those dreams are going to be yours in no time.

Visit Friends and Family

One of the nice things that you are going to enjoy about living out of a van is that you are able to go anywhere that you would like because the van is very mobile. You just have to throw all of your things inside the van and it is going to be ready to go wherever you would like it to. You might have noticed over time that your friends and family are going to become more mobile as well and soon they will be spread out throughout the whole country. You will no longer be able to reach them simply by walking down the block and conversations on the phone are not quite the same thing as seeing them face to face. Some of your friends and family might be so far away that you are only going to see them once a year or at special occasions such as weddings and reunions.

With your van, you will be able to visit any of your family and friends more often than you would be able to do if you lived in your apartment or in a house. This is due to the fact that you will have more money because you are not spending it on rent or a mortgage and because of the high mobility that comes with having a van. This mobility and more money is what is going to allow you the freedom to see your family more often and you are sure to get some big smiles out of them when they see that you have let a van in front of their homes.

These are just a few of the reasons that you might enjoy living out of a van rather than paying rent or a mortgage to someone else. It can be a great feeling when you have some money in your bank account rather than when you have to pay all of that money to someone else who is not going to help you out at all. You have so much mobility plus extra money that it is going to become a whole lot easier to get the things that you want out of life because you just take some time to live out of a van. Sure, it is going to be tough for a while and you are not going to have all of the luxuries and amenities that might come with living in an apartment or in your home, but it is going to be worth it when you are able to do some of the things that you have always dreamed about.

Whether you just plan to live in a van in order to save a few dollars and get one of your dreams to occur or if you would like to make the change more permanent, you can find a lot of things to enjoy about living out of a van.

Finding the Right Vehicle

When looking for a place to live, you do your homework pretty well, right? That should be the case when it comes to finding the right vehicle for living on the road and off the grid. Apart from one that you can be comfortable in, your vehicle of choice also needs to be something you can work with because let's face it, what use is comfort when things you need to live don't work. In this regard, vans tend to work better than other vehicles because they offer just enough size – neither too big like RVs nor too small like sedans. That being said however, you can still make something unique and useful from just about any car, truck, or vehicle.

Size Does Matter

Of primary consideration when choosing your living vehicle is the number of people that will be living in it. You can get by with less space if it just you or even one extra person but if you're considering housing your family in it, you will need considerably more space so that you aren't crowded and cramped. Trust me, small spaces can make tempers short and arguments long!

I highly recommend choosing a van for your living needs. If you're going to be the only one living in it, most vans have a good enough space for you to live comfortably. Modifying or reconfiguring it right, you can squeeze in another companion but that may be stretching it. If you're considering bringing your family, the bigger the van (or truck), the better. You can choose between panel vans, car-derived vans, mini buses, luton or box vans, ambulances and buses.

Car-derived vans are cars whose back areas are larger than most ordinary cars – like those of vans'. These types of vans are quite cheap, easy and compact to drive. Car-derived vans make for great weekend camping or out-of-town trips due to the relatively smaller living space, as their back areas aren't as big as most other vans. These are ok for 1 to 2 people and if you plan to get one of these babies for your van living adventure, you'll need to be very precise and careful in designing your living space due to their relatively smaller living spaces.

If you have more budget, you can consider getting panel vans, which are the most popular choices for off-grid van living due to their relatively spacious living spaces that are ideal for converting to medium or large camper vans. Panel vans can be bought at nice enough prices due to the relatively abundant supply of such vehicles. The rapid growth of the courier services industry in the last several years resulted in car manufacturing companies' increased production of such vans, making these babies quite abundant on the road. Since most courier service companies, especially the big ones, change their fleets every often, it shouldn't be hard to find good deals on second hand panel vans. Though the mileage on courier services' vans may be significantly higher than the average second hand panel van, these may have a good service history owing to the fact that having them break down even once in a while can be quite costly.

Chances are, most of the panel vans you'll find in the secondary market will be high-top versions, which is good because they can allow you to stand up inside. Such vans can also come in different wheelbase lengths, i.e., long, medium and short. Panel vans may be the best kind for settling down in as well as for long road trips. Even better is the fact that most people can drive it even with just a car driver's license and they're pretty much easy to maintain and drive. Panel vans are the vans of choice for accommodating up to 3 people.

A good alternative to panel vans are mini buses, many of which already have windows for a much brighter interior. So if you want to save on conversion expenses, particularly if you'd like windows for a brighter interior, this is the van to get. You can just install curtains or blinders for privacy and if you want to darken the interior from time to time. Some of them are even bigger than panel vans, which can give you more living space for comfort and amenities.

Many minibuses come with fitted seats, which can benefit you even if you don't need them. Why? You can easily take them out and earn extra cash by selling them on places like eBay. Or you can use them for setting up a dining or seating area in your living space.

On average, second-hand mini buses have less mileage compared to panel vans and as such, may be more expensive. And as with panel vans, most people can drive mini buses on a car license.

If you still find the living spaces of mini buses to be quite small or if you're considering living in your van with more than one other person, you may want to take a look at luton or box vans. These types of vans mostly have large boxes mounted on a pickup chassis at the back. Because the base pickups are made from common brands like the Ford Transit or Mercedes Sprinter, you won't have a problem sourcing spare parts for your living van.

The mounted boxes at the back in which you'll be living in are usually made from fiberglass. Although fiberglass is a very light material, it can also be a very noisy one during travel, especially on bumpy or uneven roads. They also tend to have limited insulating properties. You may want to consider insulating the box for extra strength, insulation and noise-reduction should you choose to get this kind of van for your minimalist living adventure.

Although some of these boxes have opaque ceilings that allow light to come through, it may be very noisy during rain showers. If you're going to insulate the ceiling, you'd want to leave holes for the lights to come through. And speaking of light, these boxes normally don't have windows and since the materials from which they're made are quite thin, adding windows for better ventilation and lighting can be quite a challenge. Later models have thicker walls than can be better for adding windows, if desired.

Luton vans normally have a hanging part that's ideal for converting into or adding a permanent bed to, making it a more comfortable sleeping space. Box and luton vans on average have wider spaces compared to panel vans and as such, have more space. These vans are ideal living spaces for up to 2 people. Because they're also mostly made from pickups, spare parts are quite abundant and shouldn't be a problem. However, you may need more than just a car driving license for driving these vans, depending on the area where you'll drive these in and where your driver's license was issued. Best to check first before you consider buying this kind of van for your off-grid van-living adventure.

Another alternative for your off-grid van-living adventure are ambulances. Decades ago, it was more practical to convert old ambulances into living vans due to the relatively high price of panel vans but that has changed these days, with panel vans being much cheaper than ambulances. Despite the higher price tag, however, ambulances can make for good campervan conversion particularly for those gifted with enough engineering skills, passion and enthusiasm.

These days, most ambulances are customized, i.e., adapted or purpose-built. They also have bigger engines and modified suspension systems. Most ambulances are one single unit, i.e., the front and back sections are fully integrated, and come with a hard-lined interior that's fully insulated.

Decommissioned ambulances are usually sold with all the medical equipment that they used to house removed but it can still be quite a challenge to take care of the wires and fittings that are left when converting it into your living space. They'll also probably come with 12-volts and 24-volts electricity systems, which you'll have to check to be sure.

Buying decommissioned ambulances for your off-grid van-living adventure may entail more work than the other vans because apart from the leftover wirings and fittings, you'll have to remove the blinkers mounted on top, the installed sirens and the exterior paint that screams "ambulance".

Most of them come with tinted windows though and have rear doors that easily open wide.

Although parts of ambulances are usually the same as panel van chassis, they're often more expensive because of the higher quality and custom fitting. And even though you can typically drive a decommissioned ambulance on a car driver's license, it's best to check with local authorities before buying one for your off-grid van-living adventure.

Lastly, if you want and can afford a "mansion" of a van for your off-grid living adventure, you may want to check out buses. Yes, you read that right, buses. These vehicles can give you lots of living space and can even become a truly permanent home. Its huge interior space can allow you to create "real" bedrooms and separate kitchen and living areas as well. It's like living in a small condominium but with wheels.

However, its relatively huge size can also be a disadvantage. For one, it can limit your mobility and parking space. It won't be easy driving a bus when you're already used to driving normal sized vehicles. You can easily drive along major roads that public buses often take but when it comes to residential areas that have narrower streets, you may find it really challenging. You may also be prohibited from driving on some roads and bridges due to weight and size issues. Even in some campsites, maneuverability is a great challenge for vehicles of this size.

Although used buses can be quite affordable, spare parts and fuel can be cost you an arm and a leg. And lastly, the driver's license required for buses are usually different from those of cars and a such, you may need to get another license for the purpose of driving one. Check the regulations of the places you plan to drive in prior to getting a bus for your off-grid van-living adventure.

Other Considerations When Buying Your Living Van

Another important factor with the size of the vehicle are the amenities. Do you want all of the perks you can fit in there? Or do you want to make it very primitive with just the basics in place? You also need to think about where you will be going.

If you want to be able to go to secluded places, most of which may probably be off-road, you'll need to consider a 4-wheel drive vehicle that has a high center and a heavy duty suspension system that can handle such rough terrain. Otherwise, you'll have to compromise on the places you'd like to visit or live in off-grid and stick to friendlier terrain. If you don't have an intense desire to drive to and live in secluded places with rough terrain, the stock suspensions and 2-wheel drive trains of most vans should be adequate for your living and travel needs.

Diversify as much as you can when shopping for a vehicle. Look for cargo vans – usually panel vans – that were once used by commercial companies. Many commercial panel vans only have a drivers seat, leaving the back of the van open living space. It also makes it easier and cheaper for you to re-furbish and convert it according to your living preferences. As mentioned in the previous chapter, they're typically much cheaper too compared to most other vans.

The more open or bare your van of choice is, the easier it can be to customize it in a way that will allow you to have lots of storage, such as shelves and cabinets. For example, instead of framing the bed directly on the floor between the wheel wells, frame the bed above them. This gives you access under the bed for additional storage space. If you need more than one bed, place them strategically at each of the wheel wells for maximizing space. If you have a friend who is an interior designer, you can ask for their help in planning the interiors to maximize your van living space.

Vans can often be found for sale at various sites, including social media, Craigslist, and eBay. Look around town, too, as you may see an older vehicle sitting in someone's yard that isn't being used. You never know what sort of deal you might be able to strike up with a neighbor. A good guide however is to prioritize people within your social circle who may be selling or be willing to sell the van of your choice because it lowers your risk of buying a lemon and spending more than what you budgeted due to frequent repairs.

If no one from your social circle is selling and you can't find a good deal on eBay and other social media sites, you can try placing an advertisement that says you are looking for a vehicle in major publications. Word of advice though: Try to be selective about who you buy from and what you purchase. For example, you want a vehicle that has a title. If not, be prepared for the process that you will have to go through in order to get a salvage or replacement title.

A high mileage vehicle is something that you may be able to get for a low cost. There are pros and cons to high mileage vehicles. If you plan to stay local then it might not be a bad choice. Consider too from what I wrote in the previous chapter that high mileage vehicles that used to be part of a major courier service company's fleet can be good quality ones considering that such companies are usually very anal about maintaining the good working conditions of their fleets. Just make sure to do your homework and thoroughly inspect the van you're considering buying.

It may sound trivial but the truth is, the color of the vehicle you're considering buying can be very important because it's a well-known fact that dark colors absorb heat faster than light ones and as such, choosing a dark colored van can make your living conditions hotter than you like. If you want to live cooler, choose white or other light colors for the van you plan to live in. This can make a huge difference especially if you plan to spend a great deal of time inside the vehicle during the spring and summer months when temperatures normally soar.

Another consideration is your budget. How much do you want to pay? You can get a basic vehicle that has some interior issues for a very low price. If you want a completely decked out conversion vehicle that is ready to go, it is going to cost you significantly more. Many people keep the cost low by getting a vehicle that can easily be gutted and make it into their own design. Such an approach can work well for you if you're a DIY-type of a person but if you aren't, going for vans that require less or minimal refurbishment, conversion or modifications may be more practical for you.

Speaking of getting the best price for your van, you may want to consider paying in cold, hard cash. Paying in cash can sometimes help reduce the cost of a vehicle because of the saying that a bird in the hand is better than one in the bush. What this means is that most people would be willing to lower their selling prices for the opportunity to receive the payment immediately. As such, cash payments can give you bargaining power. It also doesn't hurt to ask the seller if they will take less money than they are asking. As the great Collin Powell once said, you'll never know what you can get away with until you try. So take that minor risk of asking because the worst that can happen really is knowing they aren't willing to lower their selling price.

Now that you've carefully evaluated the kind of van you'll need to live off-grid, it's time to make a list of the items that you'll need and want for successfully living off the grid. Separate them and prioritize them. As you have money to invest, continue to add items from your list into the vehicle.

Checking Out The Van Before Buying

A vehicle that is in good working condition will make your life a lot easier. Identifying that it is in good working condition will also keep you safe. Anything you can plan for and identify beforehand will help decrease or eliminate frustrations and upset on your new adventure.

Before finalizing the deal and buying your van to convert into your mobile home, you'll need to check it out first. Never buy online without getting the chance to test drive and physically check it out first. Skip this part and you're gonna have to brace for the possibility of flushing your money and off-grid living dreams down the drain.

The important things to check are the engine, the body, chassis and transmission. Here's a checklist for the engine:

- Unusual or abnormal noise while engine is on and running is bad...really bad!

- Oil leaks in and around the engine as well as the ground where the van was last parked indicate leaks and potentially serious engine problems down the road.

- Timing belts or cam belts that are more than 60,000 miles old indicate a high risk of breaking down anytime soon. You can find this out by checking the sticker on your prospective van's engine, which indicates the latest date of change. If not, check it out in the van's service record book. If the van you're considering is already using a timing chain, that shouldn't be a problem.

- The radiator should look intact. Check to ensure it isn't falling apart at the bottom.

- If the exhaust system or muffler emits steam and smoke, beware – both aren't good signs. Diesel engines, however, do emit some smoke but it shouldn't be like the mouth of a chain smoker.

- The level of oil on the dipstick should reflect a good level. If it's low, it means the current owner isn't taking good care of the van.

-The head gasket is a very important part of the engine and if it's broken, it can be very expensive to repair or fix. To check if it's ok, take off the oil filler cap first and peek into the engine head itself. If you see some white residue, it probably means the head gasket is already blown. White residues on the oil dipstick may also suggest a blown head gasket. You can also check for a blown gasket by checking the water level in the radiator's water expansion tank or reservoir. If after test driving the van, the water in that tank has gone down significantly, it may indicate that water has gone into the engine, which means the gasket is already blown. Lastly, significant smoke and steam from the muffler when the engine is running and has already warmed up may also be indicative of a blown gasket.

-Finally, check the hoses and pipes. If the rubber hoses show cracks and the metal pipes show signs of rust that indicates a high risk that they'll break or leak soon.

To see if the van's body is in good condition, you'll need to check for rust in these areas:

-Around each and every door, particularly panel vans' hinges;

-Beneath the floor's edges;

-The arches of the wheels; and

-The roof.

Your prospective van's chassis is the key to supporting your whole mobile home, acting as it's main skeletal system. If it breaks or gives way, there goes your mobile home and van. To check if your prospective van's chassis is still in great condition or if it has a high risk for breaking down soon, do the following:

-Go under the van and run a strong stick across the chassis to probe for possible signs of severe rusting. If there are spots that give way or crumble, it means there's already severe rusting.

-Do the same around the van's wheel arches. These are a favorite tourist spot for rust because these tend to retain moisture.

-Check the van's rear and front box sections to see any indications that it may have already been involved in an accident.

Lastly, you'll need to ensure that the van's transmission is in great shape because otherwise, you run the risk of not being able to drive your home around. Here are a couple of things you can do to see if the transmission of a front-wheel drive van is still in good condition:

- -Go under the van and look for leaks in the gearbox. A little trail of light brown oil smothered with dust and dirt is normal but if you see a dark, black patch of oil dripping from it, that's bad.

- -While test-driving the van, go to a big space such as a parking area and turn the van on full steering wheel lock. If you hear some knocking-type sounds, it may indicate a damaged steering knuckle that needs to be repaired or replaced already.

If you're test-driving a rear-wheel drive van, do the following to assess the health of the van's transmission:

- -While under the van, check both the rear differential and gearbox for oil leaks.

- -Pay attention to the rear differential when test driving the van, particularly for any noise. If it's noisy, it needs to be oiled.

- -Try to grab and move the prop-shaft and if it's loose, it means it needs new bearings. Unfortunately, it's a whole assembly so you'll have to replace the whole drive shaft as well.

Accessorizing

Your own personal needs have to be assessed before you move forward with accessorizing. Do you want to go bare bones or completely self-contained living? Do you want only beds, seats for relaxing, and maybe a place to make easy meals? If so, that can be set up fairly easily. By doing your homework of identifying your actual needs and wants, segregating one from the other and prioritizing, you'll be able to increase your chances of successfully living off the grid, even if you don't have the money or the opportunity to buy everything just yet. By accurately identifying the most important needs, you'll be able to start living off the grid at the soonest possible time.

Energy

Going off-grid doesn't mean you should be living without electricity. In fact, your off-grid living adventure won't last without it. And when it comes to living in a van, you can't rely on fuel all the time because that's too expensive, environmentally un-friendly and dangerous to your health. What you'd like is a great source of energy, e.g., cheap and reliable. Among the 3 ways of generating electricity for off-grid living that I shared in an earlier chapter, solar power would be the only feasible way of consistently doing it.

Why? Obviously, wind power isn't just bulky; it's also unreliable because unlike the sun's rays, winds aren't as consistent in many places. Although using a mini-hydroelectric system is more reliable than solar (running water runs 24/7), it's only available in very few places that are often times very secluded or even prohibited.

In contrast, solar power is available practically anywhere, the system used to harness its energy is practical (portable and not as expensive) and the energy harnessed during the day can be stored for use in the evening, guaranteeing a relatively steady source of energy 24/7. As mentioned earlier, all you need are solar panels, an inverter and a good set of batteries to store energy in.

Before getting photovoltaic (solar) panels, you'll need to determine how much electricity you'll need (in voltage terms or watts) for average daily living, also called load estimates. Here's a quick guide to the daily load estimates of the some amenities or appliances you may want to have in your mobile home:

-A 9-watt fluorescent light used for 6 hours daily = 54 watts;

-A 30-watt T.V. set used for 3 hours daily = 420 watts;

-A 100-watt desktop computer used for 7 hours daily = 700 watts;

-A 110-watt Energy Star refrigerator used for 6 hours a day = 660 watts;

-A 1,400-watt microwave oven used for a total of 10 minutes daily = 233 watts;

-A small, portable 860-watt portable air conditioner used for 5 hours daily = 4,300 watts;

When you have estimated your total daily average watt-hours, you'll need to compute your battery's required capacity by dividing your daily watt hours by 12 volts (DC) and multiplying by 4 to get the battery's capacity in Ah. This capacity allows you to have a reserve of 1 day's worth of electricity just to be sure. Better yet, allow some legroom for potential increases in energy consumption.

Now that you have an idea of how much power you'll need daily, you can determine the size and number of solar panels you'll need based on their wattages, which can range from 100 to 320 watts. Check out your friendly neighborhood electronics store to help you determine how many solar panels of particular sizes you'll need and how to install them on your van home, including the battery and inverter.

Cooking

Most of your cooking can be set up outside of the vehicle. In fact, it's highly recommended that you do your cooking outside as much as possible. Options for these those that we've discussed earlier: the Crisis Cooker and rocket stoves that can easily fit in your van and are portable enough to use at a campsite or just about anywhere outdoors. For your water-heating needs, consider investing in a Hot Water Rocket that was discussed in an earlier section.

Although many camping sites areas have fire bans so you don't have to be dependent on setting a fire, you'll still need a safe and practical alternative such as the 2 above-mentioned cookers that can be used even when in places where there are no fire bans because the burnt materials used to generate heat are contained inside. And remember, you won't be living in campsites all the time, right? Unless that is your plan, of course.

Oh, another neat device to have in your home van for those times it's practically impossible to cook outside is the Burton Digital Stove To Go. This cooker, which retails for about $45, can reach temperatures that can go as high as 350 degrees Fahrenheit and it comes with a nice tray for steaming fish, dumplings or even veggies. But wait...there's more! It also has a cool recipe book to help you figure out the many different and practical ways to cook delicious food in the comforts of your home van. The only catch is that it's a relatively slow cooker, averaging about 2 hours to cook a meal.

Food Storage

Foods that have a long shelf life that don't need refrigeration can always be stored in shelves and cabinets (next section) but what about those that need to be kept cool? And what about if you enjoy having cold drinks on hand? A refrigerator, even a mini-one, may seem to be too much in terms of space, electricity and price. So what's an off-grid vagabond like you to do? The solution: The Wagan Personal Thermo-Fridge! It can function as a mini-fridge or a food warmer and this 10.5-liter fridge retails for about $110. It runs on just 12 volts and with it's size, you can maximize your home van's space as it can also easily be moved around.

Shelves

Building shelves can be a wonderful way to decorate and have room for your items. Home improvement stores have shelves ready to hang. Or purchase used shelving from second hand shops or garage sales. Just make sure these have "lips" in front to keep items from rolling off during sharp turns or sudden stops.

If you're the creative, DIY type, you can also make your own shelves for your living van. You'll need the following materials and tools:

-A ¾ inch x 6 inches x 8 feet long piece of board;

-A backsaw and miter box;

-A belt sander or sanding blocks;

-A box of 1-inch long wood screws;

-A box of machine screws with fender and lock washers;

-A countersink bit;

-A power drill with a 1/8-inch diameter metal drill bit;

-A right angle grinder with a grinding disk; and

-A set of ratchet driver with bits of screwdriver;

-Choice finish or paint;

-L-shaped wall mounts;

-Sanding belts or sand papers (extra-fine, fine and medium); and

-Wood-drilling bits that are 1/8, ¼ and ½ inch in diameter.

Before starting, determine how many shelves you'll need in your van as well as the amount of vertical clearance in between shelves. You'll also have to determine if you'll where you'll hang the shelves – along your van's walls or on the back.

After determining those important aspects, it's time to start the actual project:

-Cut your panel according to your shelves' required dimensions. For an easier time, simply use the van's length or the distances in between your van's beams.

-After cutting the board accordingly, mark the area or part of your van's wall beams that corresponds to your shelves' desired height. After marking the height, cut out 2 pieces of side support for each of your shelves, the lengths of which should be the distance between your van's floor up to the ceiling. Use miter as needed to allow for best fit and stability between the ceiling and floor.

-Mark the shelves' positions on the supports that you cut in the previous step and drill two 1/8-inch diameter holes on both left and right sides of the supports for of your shelves, which should be between the front and back (the side that's in contact with your van's wall) of the shelves. The holes should be 5 inches away from each other.

-Drill the same number of matching pilot holes – 1/8 inches in diameter each – on each of the shelves' ends. When done, countersink all the holes, including those from the previous step.

-Use the wood screws to assemble your shelves and if needed, sand screws flush them using the metal grinding disk on your right-angle grinder.

-After sanding, finish off your shelves with your choice paint, varnishes, clear acrylic coatings or stains before mounting them on your van's walls using the machine screws and wall mounts.

Cabinets

Although you can have no cabinets in your home van but having them makes it more "homey" and can offer more a more secure place to store your stuff. There are lots of styles in which you can pattern your van's cabinet but most are made from wood because they're strong, they look good, easy to make and of course, cheap. Aluminum can be an alternative material though it's pricier and may need a bit more expertise to properly handle.

You can make your cabinets in 2 ways: frameless or skinned/framed. Frameless cabinets are, as the name implies, frameless. Here, the sides of your cabinet are what make up the box. You simply join together the boards that make up all the sides of your cabinet and those boards are what give the cabinet their strength. This type of cabinet, however, tend to be heavier because of the relatively stronger – and thicker – board material needed as it's what makes for the whole thing.

Framed or skinned cabinets are those that, as the name implies also, have frames that provide the cabinet box' support and the sides are covered using panels. Since it has frames made from steel panels, solid wood or aluminum, which provide the cabinet's strength, the sides can be covered with lighter panels making the whole thing lighter than a frameless one.

When building your home van's cabinets, the obvious panels of choice are plywood because of its strength, weight, beauty and ability to resist warping and moisture. Although you can use solid wood too, which is considered higher-end material, it's more expensive, heavier and prone to warping.

When it comes to securing your home van's cabinets, corner clamps are a great help. These can easily and quickly hold together 2 wood panels at a perfect angle of 90 degrees and even allows you to adjust the joint of the 2 panels before screwing or gluing them together to make your cabinet box. As a result, you can build your cabinet boxes faster.

And speaking of piecing together your cabinet boxes, pocket screws are the best way to do it. They're easy to use and can hold your cabinet boxes together strongly. To maximize your efficient use of these screws, it's best you use these together with a pocket screw jig. With it, you can create "pockets" in which you can place the screws to join the wood panel pieces together to make your cabinet boxes.

Oh, and don't forget to use latches for your cabinets to keep them securely closed and prevent the contents from spilling over during sharp turns or sudden stops as well as unauthorized entry by small animals. Magnetic latches are poor choices for your home van. Better choose the bolt-type ones to ensure that your cabinets' doors won't easily pop open.

Receiver

A receiver or trailer hitch is another consideration. With it, a cargo carrier can then be attached to the vehicle, which can be a great place for storing coolers, stoves, propane, etc. Having a cargo carrier can help you maximize the room inside your home van while still having a safe location for everything you need outside it.

There are many kinds of trailer hitches designed for specific kinds of trailers and applications. If you decide to invest in a cargo carrier, you'll need to take into consideration some factors in order to get the best trailer or receiver hitch for your van and carrier.

First, check out your van's owner's manual to learn its tongue weight (TW) and gross trailer weight (GTW) that your home van can safely tow. TW refers to the total weight that rests on your hitch while the GTW refers to the maximum weight of your cargo carrier that your van can safely tow. When you know these figures, you can then determine the best type of trailer or receiver hitch for your home van.

Water System

Unless you're willing to take a bath in public baths or the woods for the rest of your off-grid living adventure, you'll need to consider fitting a bath and toilet system for your van home. The same goes for personal waste management, a.k.a. toilet.

As mentioned earlier, one of the best ways to have your own shower system or good running water for just about anything that needs to be washed is the RinseKit. It's portable, doesn't need power and provides good enough pressure for taking a quick bath or washing stuff like dishes and the like. All you need to do is set up a "shower" section in your van for a more discrete shower and prevent water from spilling all over your van's interior.

For personal waste management, I'll refer you again to the Porta-Potti because of its portability and convenience. I think it'll be too much to use a 5-gallon bucket every time you'll need to poo or pee. Unless you're ok to use public toilets for the rest of your off-grid living adventure and that is if they're accessible to you all the time.

The great thing about these 2 devices is that they're portable and can easily be stored anywhere in your van. As such, you can just designate one separate area for either taking a bath or taking a pee or poo. This assures you of being able to take a bath and use the bathroom even if you don't have access to public ones.

If you're not up to using a small device like the RinseKit or the Porta-Potti, have the budget for something bigger and plan to create a vehicle that will have running water for the sink, shower, or toilet, you will need a water tank. There are several options for water tanks. Water tanks take up several feet of space, so that is a consideration when planning the use of water.

Some tanks hold fresh water and some hold sewer water. A fresh water tank will offer you a spot to put a water pump. They operate with a 12 volt power resource. The pump allows the water system to have pressure. It will only operate when you turn on a faucet and the rest of the time it is idle, not continually using power.

Depending on the model you select, they can be either mounted inside the vehicle with the sub floor built over them or they can be mounted underneath the vehicle. It is a good idea to think about what you will use before you design the interior of the vehicle in case you need to make room for it.

Side Doors

If you have a van, you may want to continue to access it through the side door. However, if a bed or other item needs to be placed against the door, the door can be welded shut and entrance to the vehicle would be from the driver or passenger side.

Generator

Household products in the vehicle, such as a TV or heating and cooling units, are options. Small generators are available to operate electrical items, including household appliances. Generators will take up about ¼ of the amount of space within a cargo carrier.

Many people don't want to have a generator due to the noise they make. However, newer models are very quiet. For about 1 gallon of fuel, the generator can operate for a period of 10 hours, so it is quite economical, also. That does vary some based on size.

Heating and cooling are also options. Look for a product on the market that is dual purpose for both heating and cooling. It only takes basic skills and tools to mount one in the back of a vehicle so that the area will stay warm or cool enough for comfort.

Caution: never run the vehicle for heat or air. There is the risk of carbon dioxide poisoning. Even if you have ventilation in place, carbon dioxide can still build up in the vehicle, potentially leading to unconsciousness and death.

Curtains

Curtains can add some nice touches to the vehicle. It is a good idea to use a dark color so that you can close them and block out the sunlight. In a van, a rod can be installed with long curtains behind the driver's seat area. It should be long enough to go all the way across. This can give added privacy.

Screens

Consider adding screens to the windows, allowing you to open the windows for ventilation. Screens also reduce the risk of bugs and mosquitoes getting inside. A bug zapper is another option and can be placed outside to help reduce the volume of pests. Citronella candles, used outside of he vehicle may have some effect on the reduction of bugs.

Flooring

Depending on how rustic you want the vehicle to be, you may want to consider different types of flooring. You can make it simple with rubber mats that are easy to clean. Or carpet if you want to have something soft under your feet.

If you select carpet, think about how you'll keep it clean. Using the generator to operate a small vacuum or carpet cleaner is an option. Linoleum is another option.

Carpet and linoleum require something secure underneath. Plywood or wafer boards are options to consider. Attach with self-tapping screws and then carpet or linoleum can be put in place.

Interior Walls

Wooden slats along the walls and ceiling with self-tapping screws are also a great method. This provides you with the chance to offer insulation for the winter months. Wiring can also be hidden behind it and then covered with paneling. The wooden slats offer a base to secure the screws for the paneling. You can put any color of decorative paneling you want or you can pick ¼ inch plywood and paint it any color you desire.

If you want to really decorate it, consider wallpaper. There are all types of designs out there to pick from. Remember, you will be living in it and seeing it all the time.

Others

The miniaturization of the many items is vast. You can get a small vacuum, washer and dryer (and you thought you were going to be scrubbing the clothes in the river!), countertop dishwasher, and even a microwave. Appliances can fit in very small places and give you some of the comforts of home that you don't want to miss out on.

Need that morning coffee? You can get a device that makes a full pot - plugs right into the cigarette lighter on your vehicle!

Of course these appliances will significantly increase the cost invested in your vehicle. Still, if it is a long term living area you can add items that will enhance the value. You can benefit from them while you use it and also have improved selling power when you are finished with it.

You also need to have a secure way to store trash. Be sure and collect and discard trash daily from your vehicle so that it won't smell.

An extra set of keys for everything inside of the vehicle as well as the lock on the vehicle should be well hidden outside of the vehicle. Make sure it isn't in a common location where it can easily be found. The keys should be secured with wire or other device so that they won't fall off when you move the vehicle.

Finally, being organized is important when you have so many items in a small space. Make sure items overhead are going to stay in place so that they don't fall on you when you walk by. Less is more in terms of what you have out in the open. By putting items upward instead of outward you will have more room.

Safety

Safety is a priority in living a van. Planning is important to ensure that the vehicle is safe at all times. Here are the areas you'll need to consider for your personal safety while living off the grid in your home van.

Wiring

I've you already bought a van to convert into your mobile home for your off-grid living adventure, one of the most important things you'll need to plan are how to power it and along with it, the electrical wiring system. Your choice of how to set up your wires is dependent on several factors like cost, the size of your van and the appliances you plan to accommodate.

If you're a novice or amateur electrician, take my advice: leave it to the pros. Spending money for their expertise is a good investment if you're not skilled at wirings and stuff.

Whether you'll be the one to install the van's wirings or a professional electrician, insist on using flexible, 3-core main cables for your home van's electric needs. Compared to the average domestic cable, 3-core main cables are composed of many fine strands of copper that provides more flexibility for your wires, reducing the risk of becoming brittle and eventually, breaking. This also gives your electrical wiring system more firmness that may provide beneficial considering the demands of an electrical wiring system of a moving vehicle.

Fire Safety

Motorhome fires can be quite rare but it doesn't mean you should take it easy when it comes to fire safety. However remote the chances of a fire breaking out in your camper van, the damage can be quite high or even fatal if it does happen. As such, one the most important safety features to have in place in your van home is at least one fire extinguisher and fire blanket.

Fire extinguishers and blankets are very important for any home, be it a mobile or traditional one. Fires are classified from Classes A to F, which corresponds to the type of material that's burning.

-Class A: Solids like plastics, wood and paper;

-Class B: Flammable liquids like oil, petrol and paraffin;

-Class C: Flammable gasses like methane, butane and propane;

-Class D: Metals like titanium, magnesium and aluminum;

-Class E: Electrical apparatus (electrical fire); and

-Class F: Substances such as fat and cooking oil.

Fire extinguishers are classified as water, foam, dry powder, CO_2 and wet chemical, which are used for specific fire classes. Water fire extinguishers are the most popular, possibly because they're the cheapest, and are suitable for Class A fires only. Foam fire extinguishers are more versatile compared to water but are pricier. It's suitable to put out Classes A and B fires. Dry powder fire extinguishers – popularly known as the multi-purpose fire extinguisher – is best suited for putting out Class B fires but can also be used for Classes A and C fires. There are special powder extinguishers for Class D metal fires. For electrical fires (Class E), CO2 fire extinguishers are ideal, which can also be used for Class B fires. For putting out Class F fires (oil and fat), wet chemical fire extinguishers are the most suitable ones to use.

Which one to buy? Well, consider the materials inside your camper van and choose the appropriate kind of extinguisher. If you're on a budget, consider what are the most abundant materials that may be burned inside and choose the appropriate fire extinguisher for it.

After purchasing your fire extinguisher, make sure to mount it securely so that it can't roll around when you drive the vehicle. It needs to have a designated stop so that you always know where it is in an emergency.

For smaller fires or incipient ones (just starting out), you can use fire blankets to put them out. Fire blankets are "blankets" or sheets made of materials that are fire retardant and are placed over such kinds of fires in order to smother them until extinguished. Most of them are usually made of fiberglass and in some cases, Kevlar. As with normal blankets and sheets of cloth, these can be folded in a way that they're easy to store in drawers or cabinets and can be quickly released when there's a fire.

Fire blankets can withstand up to 900-degree temperatures. When they're placed over small, incipient fires, fire blankets work by preventing oxygen from feeding the small, incipient fires – choking off the supply of oxygen that can make the fire grow bigger.

Apart from extinguishers and blankets, you can further the risk of a fire breaking out in your home van by making sure you have at least one smoke detector and one carbon dioxide detector in the van. This will help to ensure you are alerted if there are any issues and alert you to get out of the vehicle quickly. The batteries in such devices should be changed every six months.

Prevention is always much better than cure so if you plan to have a stove, water heater, or appliances inside of the vehicle, they will need to be checked regularly. Review all of the cords for any damages.

Having a vent in the roof of the vehicle is highly recommended. When you have such items in a confined space, there is the risk of fumes building quickly and consequently, possible combustions or fires. Putting a vent or vents on your van can help minimize this risk.

Animal Protection

No, I'm not talking about your taking care or protecting animals. I'm talking about you protecting yourself from them, especially in the wild where you may choose to camp or live for a while. Carry bear spray, pepper spray, and other items for protection.

Take good care to seal and store your foods well, especially when in the wild. This is because some wild animals like bears can open locks so if they smell food, they can get in.

They can also break glass if they are hungry and determined. As mentioned earlier, the prevention card always trumps the cure one.

Criminal Protection

Animals aren't the only ones you'll need to protect yourself from. You'll also need to think of safety in terms of other people getting into the vehicle – burglars, robbers or just about any person with a really nasty plan against you and your possessions. In this regard, sturdy doors and quality locks are a must have you're your safety and protection.

Motorhomes, like your van home, are more vulnerable to theft and breaking in compared to regular or normal homes for several reasons. First, it isn't possible to install motorhome alarms that can be linked to a private security service or the local police. Another reason is the basic structure of the motor home – they're not really built to be a fortress against thieves. Compared to a normal home, it's much easier to break through an automobile's doors or windows and due to the thin walls, thieves can easily inflict serious damage and allow them to break in. A third reason why motorhomes are more vulnerable is mobility. Because most residents of motorhomes travel frequently, they don't have the luxury of time to coordinate and work with local police – and thieves know and exploit this. Lastly, motorhome drivers who do a lot of travel naturally aren't as knowledgeable of the areas they travel to and live in, which increases the risks for being broken into.

One of the best ways to defend your mobile piece of heaven is making sure you'll be able to lock the vehicle when you are inside so that no one can get in without your permission. You should also be able to securely lock it up when you venture away from the vehicle. In this regard, high quality and very tough door locks are a great investment.

Another way of protecting your van home is by knowing it very well. Start by conducting an inventory of all the things you have in and outside your van home, which can prove to be very useful for police assistance and insurance claims, in case thieves do break in and ransack your little piece of mobile heaven. It's also a good idea to take pictures of more important stuff like your computer or TV set and attach these photos to the inventory list you made. Do this every six months.

Another good way to secure your van is to make it stand out from the crowd or easily identifiable. Apart from painting it with a unique color (hot pink, anyone?), you can also consider sticking clearly visible identification marks, designs or texts on the body or on the roof (for easier police visibility from a helicopter if ever). Take photographs of it so that the police officers can easily identify it on the road in case it gets stolen.

Lastly, never leave your van home without turning the engine off and taking the keys with you. Many motorhome thefts happened when drivers leave the vehicle with the engine running and waiting thieves immediately take advantage of the situation to hijack and run-off with the vehicle.

Essential Kits

Living off-grid, especially on the road, is significantly riskier than living in a normal, stationary home. As such, living in a van and off the grid will require that you prepare kits that will help you manage those risks well, should they occur.

One such kit is the first aid kit, which is what you'll need to use should you or your companion get injured or fall sick. A good first aid kit for your off-grid, van living should include:

-Bandages;

-Crepe bandages for taking care of sprains;

-Different sizes of dressing pads to help take care of minor wounds;

-Gauzes (sterile);

-Insect bites and blisters cream;

-Insect repellents;

-Ointments or creams to clean and sooth minor skin burns;

-Petroleum jelly;

-Sunscreens;

-Tablets for purifying water;

-Triangle-shaped bandages to make slings in case of arm injuries; and

-Waterproof and strong plasters.

Have some medical supplies on hand in case you need them. This includes common ailments such as a headache or back pain. Eye drops, eardrops, sore throat medication, allergy pills, anti-rash cream, and anything else you can think of that you may need should be on hand.

If you take prescription medications, you certainly need to make sure you have enough for your time away. Store all medications in a dry location and away from the sunlight. A small lunchbox that is insulated can be a very good option.

Always have a well-stocked first aid kit. You'll need plenty of supplies for a variety of problems and the better stocked it is, the better you can take care of possible sicknesses and injuries.

Aside from the first aid kit, you'll need to assemble a survival kit for living on the road and off the grid. The survival kit is one that can help you survive in case a major catastrophe happens in the city or locality you're located in. The first aid kit is, technically, part of the survival kit. Other items that you should consider including in your survival kit include:

-Cooking Pot;

-Emergency blankets;

-Emergency Food /Dehydrated Food;

-Hand Saw;

-LED Strobe Flashlight and Extra Batteries;

-Lighters, or Waterproof Matches;

-Map and compass;

-Pocket Knife;

-Rope;

-Small Mirror;

-Water Supply;

-Weather Appropriate Clothing/Rain Gear; and

-Whistle.

You can modify this list to suit your particular needs and the places where you'll plan to go and live. However, these items should form the core of your survival kit and you may add others you think are needed or would like to have such as fishing poles and lines, plastic trash bags and flares.

A CB radio is a good idea if you will be in locations where you aren't going to have cell phone reception. This type of communication can help you to get assistance quickly. The more remote the area, the more important it is to have a CB radio in place.

Make sure the CB you obtain has the WX weather channel available. You'll want to be aware of any weather alerts or evacuations in the area. Weather updates and advisories will only be for your given location, as the signal will bounce off of towers in closest proximity to you.

Hand held CB radios can be cared with you when you are away from your vehicle, allowing you to get updates quickly. Getting alerts as soon as possible will allow you make the decision to find shelter where you are or to make the distance back to your vehicle for shelter.

Flares are a good idea because they can be seen from a long distance. If you can't communicate with your CB radio or the cell phone, flares can send a message quickly. This type of backup plan should only be used in the event of an emergency.

Check In Regularly

For safety reasons, its best to always make sure someone knows where you will be and when you will be returning. You may have limited resources to connect with the important people in your life, but check in on a regular basis. Someone in your life should have a good idea of how to find you if you don't check in. This will help ensure that someone will come looking for you at a given point in time if you haven't been heard from.

That's why it's essential to at least have a CB radio or a satellite phone on stand by. These 2 devices can help you check in on loved ones even in the most remote places on earth. It'll allow you to get help quickly too, in case something happens to you in a very remote place.

Insurance

If you have the vehicle insured, make sure the coverage will also include the contents of the vehicle. Scrimping on insurance may prove to be more costly on your end should something bad happens to you and your van home. Aside from doing an inventory of the stuff you have in and outside the van (as discussed earlier), taking digital photos, attaching them to your inventory and keeping copies of them at a safe location (if you have mobile internet and access to cloud storage, that's great) outside the van can help you access them quickly should you have a theft, water damage, or you experience a fire and file for insurance.

Don't Play With Fire

If you want to minimize the risk of burning your mobile home, then avoid using candles or lanterns in your vehicle because they are dangerous. You can opt for some led lamps (if you have a solar powered electric system, including a battery) or solar powered lights instead. For the latter, place the lights outside during the day to charge the batteries and use them at night inside the vehicle. This is a great idea if you don't have electricity.

Flameless candles can also help create the atmosphere you want without risk. Flameless candles don't get hot and will continue to offer hours and hours of light when turned on. These candles, also known as LED candles, are electric alternatives to traditional wick candles. Normally, these are used as decorative lighting gadgets and they come in many sizes, colors and shapes. Their use of a tiny bulb instead of a wick that's set on fire makes them a great alternative to regular candles due to both no risk of burning and being smokeless. And because these are LED, they are very energy efficient.

Some flameless candles have timers on them. Will you be returning to the vehicle after dark? Just set the timers so that they will come on at a given time. The timer can also give others in the area the idea that someone is in the vehicle when it is empty. This can deter the risk of theft or other crimes.

Rotation Expiration Prevention

One of the risks you'll also have to manage when living on the road – that you also manage when living in a normal home – is the risk of using or eating expired items. A good way to minimize this risk is to rotate your supplies so that they can be consumed prior to expiration and not after it. When you buy new items, move other items forward and put the most recent ones at the back. It'll also be a good idea for you to create and update a maintenance calendar for your mobile home. Be sure to keep plenty of various size batteries on hand for small devices, such as flashlights.

Testing Your Mobile Home

Before taking off on your off the grid, van living adventure, you have to make sure that everything is well with your mobile home. If you have installed anything that requires plumbing, such as a shower, toilet, or sink, they will need to be tested for leaks. The time to find out that you have a leak isn't when you are out at a camp sight! Try to identify all problems before leaving.

Be sure to test any electrical wiring for your appliances. You want to make sure appliances aren't getting too hot or at risk for overheating. Check for any short circuits. Also, check to make sure there isn't an electricity overload that will shut your power down or cause a fire hazard.

Test your smoke detector and carbon detector to make sure they are in working order and have fresh batteries. If you have any stoves or other cooking items, use them in the vehicle prior to leaving in order to make sure the ventilation system is properly set up. If you can cook in the vehicle without the detectors being set off, then that is a very good indicator that the vehicle is properly ventilated, and safe.

All vehicles have specific weight ratings measuring what they can carry on each axle. Avoid getting too much weight on one end of the vehicle; try to evenly distribute it as much as possible. During the building process, if you have a place close by that has a commercial scale for vehicles (grain elevator), take the vehicle there to be weighted at regular intervals. You'll want to weigh the front axles and the back axles separately. This helps you to see that the front and the rear are balanced.

Check the tires to make sure they have enough pressure and quality trend. Regularly check the air pressure in the tires. Also, be sure the spare tire has air in it and that you know how to change a flat tire.

Check the lighting system on the vehicle. Test the blinkers to make sure they work as they should. Do the headlights and the bright lights work on the vehicle like they should? All are of the brakes lights working?

When was the last time the oil was changed? Are the fluids full including antifreeze, transmission fluid, and windshield wiper fluid? All of this is important so that you aren't going to end up stranded with problems that you have to try to fix on the side of the road. You need the basics of the vehicle to operate well for you so that you can actually rely on the vehicle to get you to and from the intended destination.

It may sound silly, but make sure the gas gauge works! On older vehicles it may not. If it doesn't, write down the mileage each time you get gas and estimate on the low side how many miles you can safely travel before you need to fuel up again.

Does the speedometer work? If not, you will have a harder time obeying posted speed limit laws. It isn't enough to just be able to keep up with the flow of traffic! That isn't going to get you off the hook with a traffic ticket or speeding in a construction zone!

If you have a trailer hitch, ensure that it is secure and make sure the lights on the trailer are in working order. If you have items that are tied to the back or the top of the vehicle they need to be securely in place. When you stop along your route, double check them as they can work loose with the ride.

Keep some basic tools with you on site so that you can do minor repairs if you do run into snags along the way. Even if you test everything, you need be prepared for what could occur down the road. And don't forget insurance in case of a break-in or accident.

Selecting Your Destinations

It has been said that failing to plan is planning to fail. The same can be said with your living off-grid in a van. And one important thing to plan is your destination. Now that you have a working mobile home, its time to select the places you want to go to in your mobile home.

Local Ordinances And Regulations

After short-listing the places you want to visit, you'll need to check out their local ordinances and regulations because you may get into trouble without meaning to. In some places, for example, you can't park your vehicle by the river. Other places may allow that but for a limited period of time only, which means you can't really live there.

Some places put a restriction on fishing, which can be quite a bummer if you're looking forward to doing it either for recreation or necessity (food). In other places, campfires aren't allowed so if you're only option for cooking food, heating water and warming up is an open fire, you might be forced leave sooner than you wish or end up renting a place, which defeats the purpose of living off the grid.

Other areas don't restrict the number of people or campers in an area and if one of your preferences is privacy, you may be utterly disappointed after a long drive if you didn't do your homework.

Be sure to investigate any area you plan to stay in so that you don't get run off by local law enforcement for violating the laws. You don't want to get a fine or a court date for not paying attention to these established rules and laws.

Topography

You'll also need to check out your preferred destination's topography, both before going there and as soon as you arrive there. Doing so helps you minimize the risk of figuring in an accident, particularly to natural disasters. If staying by a river for example, always park your vehicle above the highest water line for the river. Flash flooding can occur very rapidly and you need to make sure your vehicle will be out of harms way. Don't make the assumption that you will have the time to move it! Flooding can happen in the middle of the night when you are asleep. Remember the earlier reference to the importance of a weather radio.

Weather Conditions

Weather conditions can spell the difference between an enjoyable stay in your choice destination and a really bad one. As such, weather conditions certainly need to be a factor when considering a location. Some areas around the river can easily get into the triple digits in the summer months. Inside of the vehicle, it can be too hot and you don't want to rely on the generator all the time. Other locations are just too bitter cold for winter outdoor living, so you'll want to plan accordingly.

Find a location with temperatures that are moderate for the time of year you plan to be there. If you are going to be living in the vehicle for a period of time, then you'll need to look at the seasonal changes that could influence your decision. You'll want to consider areas of high wind, hail, or tornado risks, not just extreme temperatures.

A dry, level spot will be important when parking your vehicle. Carry several blocks of wood or bricks to slide behind the front tires and in front of the back tires to help prevent the vehicle from slipping or rolling.

Supplies Needed

Before you go and live in a van, you might need to make sure that you have all of the supplies that are necessary to ensure that you are getting set up in the right way. You are going to be living in your van so it is important that you get all of the supplies ahead of time so that you can be comfortable. It is an option to go to the store, but if you are trying to live out of the van in order to save up some money, it can sometimes be a better idea to use some of the supplies that you already have.

No matter where you get the supplies that you are going to need, you should keep them on hand so that you are prepared to live as comfortable as possible. Some of the supplies that you might need include:

-Clothes—the first thing that you need to make sure to take with you is plenty of clothes. You are going to be living out of the van so you must make sure that you are taking enough clothes with you to last at least long enough until you have time to do laundry, which is usually a week or so in between. You will probably have to go and visit a laundry mat to do your clothes unless you are able to park somewhere that allows you to hang your clothes out of the window or on a homemade clothesline.

Keep plenty of shirts, pants, socks, underwear and any other articles of clothing that you are going to need in order to be properly dressed for work. If you are dressing up for work, you should invest in some hangers or some hanging bags to keep the clothes out of the way and wrinkle free; also, keep the clothes laying out flat where they are not going to be harmed or get all wrinkled in between work times.

-Laundry equipment—just because you are living in a van does not mean that you should avoid doing laundry on a regular basis. Some of the most successful van dwellers are those that are able to show up to work and their other engagements and no one can tell because they are able to keep everything clean and tidy. You should be able to do the same with just a little bit of work and visiting a laundromat during the weekends. Make sure that you bring all of the things that you need in order to keep your laundry clean and fresh including laundry detergent, fabric softener, stain cleaners, fabric sheets, and anything else that you might need.

-Personal hygiene supplies—even though you are living out of a van does not mean that you should let your personal hygiene go out the window. You are not going to be saving any money in the process of living out of your van if you lose your job because you smell bad or your teeth are falling out. You need to keep up your personal appearance while you are living out of the van so that you still are presentable and can feel your very best as well. There are a lot of hygiene supplies that you are going to be able to choose from and it is kind of up to your personal preferences. Basically you should bring along any of the supplies that you would use in your own home, with perhaps some more cologne so that you do not smell bad from living in such a little space.

Some of the hygiene items that you should consider bringing include hair brush, toothbrush, toothpaste, deodorant, cologne or perfume, razors, shaving cream, towels, shampoo, soap, lotion, contact solution, contacts, glasses, and anything else that you need in order to get all nice and up kept for your work or other engagements.

-Phone—you should make sure that you have a good working phone on you at all times when you are living in a van. You are not going to have one location that is available to you when you are living out of a van like you would if you were living in a home or an apartment. You might also find that if you are in a van you might have to park in some places that are out in the middle of nowhere and you will not be able to get help right away if you need it. You should get a nice phone that gets good reception and that is going to work no matter where you are going to go. This is going to help others get in contact with you if they need to or if you need help you will be able to get it right away.

Phone charger—in addition to having your phone working well, you should make sure that you have a working phone charger that can be used at any time. It is often best to get one that works in a vehicle so that you are able to keep your phone charged up while you are traveling around or heading to work. It is not going to do you any good to have the phone if it is always dead and you do not have a way to charge it back up. You should make sure that the charger is working well and that it is able to work well with your phone so that you are prepared no matter what.

-Food—if you are living out of your vehicle, it is a good idea to pick out food that you can eat while there. You do not want to waste a lot of money going to out to eat each night; this is going to end up costing you a lot more money in the long run than keeping your home or your apartment and eating at home. You are going to need to learn how to shop so that you can get the food that you need at the grocery store and that you can eat out of your van. You might find that you have to go to the grocery store each week due to the limits on space compared to your old home, but this should not be too difficult.

Finding the types of food that you need in order to stay full and to not have it go out and get bad can sometimes be difficult. Try to find foods that are not going to spoil quickly, such as those that are going to be packaged or that need to be kept frozen. If you want to have fresh meat, this is possible in the van, but you will probably need to go and get it on the night that you want to serve it in order to avoid it going rotten. This would be the same with fresh fruits and vegetables. It is a good idea to do a little research in order to find the foods that are going to work out the best for your needs and try to only get as much fresh foods as you are able to eat in a few meals time so that you are not becoming wasteful and having to throw it out.

-Emergency kit—having an emergency kit on hand is a great idea. You might be out away from the store or other conveniences at some times when you are living in a van, especially if you are on the road and traveling to see the people and the places that you have missed in life. You might not be anywhere near a store that is going to have bandaids or other supplies when you need them so it is a good idea to keep them on hand in case you find that you need them. There are a lot of different things that you can pack into your emergency kit. Some people might choose to purchase one that is already made up. This is a great idea because you already know that all of the things that you are going to need will be right there ready for you to use and they come in a nice container that is easy to store. If you feel like there is not a kit that has these things that you would like, then it is a good idea to create the kit that you would like. There are a lot of different supplies that you are able to put into your kit. Some good things to include would be Bandaids, antiseptic, wipes, soap, bug spray, suntan lotion, poison ivy cream, cough syrup, Tums, and anything else that you think might be of use.

-Bedding supplies—since you are going to be living out of your van it makes sense to think that you will need some bedding supplies for when you are sleeping. You should bring anything that you think is going to be helpful when you are living inside. This could include pillows, sheets and blankets. If you are able to fit it into your van you could bring along a small cot that is easy to full up because you will want to save some room in the back. If the van is large enough you might find that putting a mattress is helpful so that you can be more comfortable. It is up to you if there are more bedding materials that you will be able to bring along in order to be comfortable in the van.

-Winter supplies—at some point you are going to need to have some winter supplies that are readily available when that season comes along. It can get really cold in a van and you will not have easy access to the heat that you were used to in your old home or apartment. Sure you are able to leave the heat on at some point, but it would waste a lot of your batter and gas if you leave it on all of the time. If you are going to live in the van during the summer, you could wait until later to get your winter supplies in order to save some money.

There are a lot of different winter supplies that you should make sure to have on hand. Some of these things would include extra blankets, coats, sweaters, sweat pants, snow pants, hats, gloves, scarves, and winter boats. Depending on the things that you have in your van and how much space you have in your van, you might be able to add in a little space heater that can help to keep you warm. Make sure that you pick a spot that you can park that is going to make it easier to charge up your battery so that it does not die out on you.

-Storage—one thing that people forget to bring about with them when they are living in a van is some storage. You are going to need to have some places in order to put your food, your equipment, your clothes, your bedding, and some of the other things that you are bringing along. It is not a good idea to just leave all of your stuff out and around the van because this is going to make a huge mess and could cause a lot of issues with room or if you are driving around. One of the best things that you can do is pick out a van that has the storage under the seats and in your floors of the van. This will allow you to put all of your stuff out of the way while allowing a lot of extra room in the van at the same time. If you do not have a van that is able to do this, you will have to find some other form of storage that you are able to use in order to get all of the stuff put away. You can get some little storage units or even plastic containers with lids that allow you to get everything out of sight and out of the way. Make sure that you get ones that are going to allow you to have room in the vehicle but still hold all of the things that you have.

-Car TV—if you are planning on living in the van for a long time, you might find that it can get boring at nights or when you are not at work. Of course, you could go and visit with friends and family on some nights or you might even have a work function to go to. But just like when you were living in your apartment, you might find that you would like to have a few nights that are all your own; nights that you do not have to go out and find ways to entertain yourself. You are not going to want to just sit in the dark and be left alone to your own thoughts. You could bring along a small car TV that can help with this. You can use the one that is in your van, bring along an old small one that you can hook up to an outlet, or pick out a TV that is meant to go in your car and can hook in to the cigar outlet in the vehicle. In some of the areas where you are stopping, you may be able to pick up a little bit of reception in order to catch a few of your favorite shows at night or even the news and the weather. You could also use it to watch a few of your favorite movies.

-Movies—if you are going the route of bringing a car TV along on the trip with you, it is a good idea to bring a few movies along as well. This is going to allow you to watch something on the TV without having to worry about whether you are getting reception to cable or not, which is something that is going to happen if you are always on the move. Pick out some of your favorite movies in order to be entertained or you can go and buy a few new ones to enjoy for the first time. If you are worried about having enough room in your car in order to hold the videos, you should bring along a CD case and just place the DVD's inside. You can then get rid of the cases that come with the DVD's and in turn save a lot of room. If you are really cramped on space in your vehicle, you may want to go another route and choose to go with some rentals. You can borrow them for a few days whenever you are interested in watching something, you are always going to have something new to watch, and you are able to return them at any time so that they are not taking up more room in your car when you are low on the space.

-Books—if you are someone who likes to read you might find that bringing along some books is a great way to entertain yourself while living in a van. You should also make sure to bring along a nice source of light so when it gets dark you are not going to have to worry about straining your eyes or getting bored. If you are worried about the amount of space that you have, your library is going to be the best bet for you. This is going to allow you to get a constant stream of books without having to take up a lot of space in your van.

-Camping Cooking utensils—you are going to have to cook some meals when you are living out of the van. You do not want to worry about going to the store all of the time and it is not very often that you are going to be able to pick up a full meal that is already made without having to put something together. You will find that having some camping cooking utensils on hand can make it all a little bit easier. This can be especially true if you are choosing to stay at a designated paring spot because you are going to have more access to camping supplies in order to cook with. It is often not a good idea to put a stove in your vehicle because it is easier to catch on fire so you might have to find a place that can provide this to you instead.

These are just a few of the things that you should bring along with you in order to properly live in your van. You are going to have to make the best judgment for the things that you must use in order to survive out of the van. Each person is going to find that there are different things that they need in order to be successful and it is going to change depending on what they think is important or what they think they are able to get on without.

It is important to remember that you are not going to have a lot of extra room in your van in order to bring a lot of extra things along so you should try and only pick out the things that are the most important and which are going to be able to help you the most.

Where to Go

When you are living in a van, you might be curious about where you should go or where you will be able to park the van. You do not want to leave it in an area that it is going to get towed and cost you a lot of money to take care of, but you also do not want to leave it in the middle of nowhere that is going to get you hurt or on a side of the street and get in trouble because you look like a creeper. While there are a lot of choices when it comes to your parking spot, it is going to take some careful planning on your part in order to get it all right. This choice of parking spot is going to be the most critical and difficult one that you will need to make and you should make it as soon as possible so that you are not stuck moving from place to place and feeling like you do not belong.

Some of the things that you will have to take into consideration when you are choosing a spot will include avoiding the police, the quality of sleep that you will be able to get, how secure the place is, and how safe it is. It can become even more difficult due to the fact that many communities are passing laws that state how living out of a van is illegal so you will need to find a place that can keep you hidden. This can make the whole thing a big challenge.

This chapter is going to spend some time discussing the various spots that you can park in order to be safe, not go against the law, and still enjoy the life that you want living out of a van.

The Wilderness

There are no laws that state that you are not able to bring your van out to the wilderness and sleep there if you would like. And from the view of a good night of sleep, security, and safety, you are not going to find a better choice than staying in a location that is heavily forested and many miles away from other forms of civilization and parked next to the nearest river or creek. You are soon going to find that staying in this area is going to provide you with a surrounding that is really serene and with gentle sounds that come from the flowing water. Most people find this is some of the best sleep that they have ever gotten and you are going to feel rested and at peace without having to worry about being parked in the wrong place. There are quite a few locations where you will be able to do this as long as you are in the right part of the country.

Some great regions include the central parts of the Appalachians, Pacific Northwest, and the Rocky Mountain region. You might find that other parts of the country are not as inviting as they do not provide as much forested wilderness for you to enjoy so you may have to rely on some of the other options that will be provided later in this chapter. There is a downside that you might find when you are staying in these areas which is that it is very remote and far away from other things. This means that you are going to be a long way from many of the conveniences that come with modern life, grocery stores, gas stations, friends and family, and even work. If you plan to still go back and forth to work, this might not be the solution for you since you will spend a ton of money going back and forth and on gas.

Desert and Plains

Another area that you may want to consider is the plains and desserts of the country. There is a lot of land like this in the country, in fact there is probably over half the country that would fit this description, which might be difficult for someone who lives in the city to imagine. You can often choose to still be close to other forms of civilization while still being out and away. This will allow you to get some of the community atmosphere that you would like in order to not get lonely but you will still be alone and get away from the noise and the prying eyes of the police.

City Camping: Residential

If you have decided to live out of a van and you are from the city, you are going to be stuck with three locations that you can choose from. These will include industrial, commercial, and residential areas. You are not going to have the option to stay in the desert, plains, of the wilderness because these locations are just too far away from the city and you will never be able to afford the gas much less have time to go back and forth. The first area that you might choose to do is camping in a residential area. This is a good place to start because you will be able to blend in pretty easily to the other cars that are staying on the street at night. It is going to be important that you have a vehicle that is easy to blend in otherwise others might notice and are going to report you. You will need to make sure to stay away from some of the wealthier neighborhoods that you live near because they will not be likely to leave their cars out on the street and so they will quickly notice when yours is there.

Be sure and take a look at the crime rate in the area that you want to park. Some areas with a higher crime rate can be dangerous because you will run the risk of your van being stolen if you are away or someone breaking in. If you have chosen a cargo van in order to live in, it is best to stay away from most of the residential areas and choose somewhere else because it is really difficult for this kind of vehicle to fit in.

City Camping: Commercial Areas

You might find that businesses and retail outlets are great places that you will be able to park your van in order to lie.

This is especially a good idea if you are living out of a box van, cargo van, or other commercial like vehicle because they will fit more and look like they belong. When you are stuck in a city, it is important that you are being as stealthy as possible, these commercial locations are the best option for you. You do not just have to have a big vehicle. If you park in a lot that has overnight hours or stockers that work at night so that you are able to fit in a little bit better. You might also want to consider putting some sort of disguise on your van. For example, if you are parking near a plumbing supply store you can get some magnets and PCV pipe to put on the van in order to make it blend in a little bit better.

City Camping: Industrial Sectors

These are usually the last places that people will want to choose to park in, but if you have no other safe options they can work as well. These zones are usually dirtier and noisier than other parts of the city which means it is more likely that someone is going to see you come and go because the plant has operations that are 24 hours a day. These areas also have the highest crime rates of the whole city so you are more likely to get robbed or have stuff stolen if you leave the van for any amount of time. It is usually best to avoid these places unless you are stuck for anywhere else to go.

Summary: The Best Parking Place?

This is often just going to depend on your own personal preferences. Some people want to be in the city so that they can get to work really easy and others would prefer to have the peace and quiet of being a little bit out of town in order to not get caught. Some people find that living out of their vans in the city is the best for them because they like to be near their friends and family and do not want to be out in the middle of nowhere if something bad happens to them. Or they might like to be close to work so that they are not commuting so far and wasting as much gas. On the other hand, there are others who might really enjoy the fact that they can almost camp in the wilderness and get the peace and quiet that they have been looking for in their lives. Sometimes it is going to depend on the area of the world that you live in and how much traveling you are going to do while you are living out of a van. For example, if you live in a city it is going to be difficult to find somewhere that has secluded wilderness that you can stay in that is not hours away; if you live in the Midwest or the South, there is a lot more of this area that you can choose from and you might have fewer choices when it comes to city living. There are a lot of options that you can choose from which can be some of the fun. Make sure you pick an area that is quiet and that will keep you safe, regardless of where you choose.

Here are a few other strategies that you can try out when you are looking for a place to park your van.

Planning on leaving:

-Park in an area that has a lot of visibility so that you are less likely to be robbed.

-If you plan on leaving each day, you are going to open up a lot more options for where you are able to stay. If you are there for a day or two no one is likely to notice that you are there and you can stay without anyone bugging you. It seems like the longer that you are in a place the more likely it is that others are going to notice that you are staying there because they will begin to recognize your vehicle and might report you. Before picking an area you need to decide if it is going to be a permanent spot, one that you are going to stay for some amount of time, or one that you plan to leave the next day.

Planning on staying for some time:

-If you have someone who can help you out, you can use them to park the van for you anywhere that you would like as long as it allows overnight parking. To someone who might be observing, it is going to look like your friend just parked the van and then left it. If you have a barrier in the van you can then get in the van to start with, although you should be careful to not arouse suspicion, or you can do the transfer away from eyes and then go to the parking spot.

-Take the time to park in the early morning hours and then shut the doors as if you left the van. This way people will just think that you are shopping or that you are staying at one of the houses that are there.

-Park in a way so that no one is able to see the entrance to your van. For example, if you get out of one of the side doors, make sure that door is not visible from the street.

This will allow you to get in and out of the van easier because no one is going to notice when you do so.

-Park your van so that it looks like you are going to leave it overnight and then come back later. You should always be wary of who might be watching you. Do not try this in the residential areas because it is really hard to tell who is watching you unless it is late at night.

-Park near other vans, especially those that look similar to yours. This is going to allow you to blend in more with the crowd and people are less likely to notice you.

-In the wintertime you should make sure to park near the sunlight. This is going to help the van stay warmer during the cold. During the summer you should do the opposite and park in the shadows. This is going to allow the van to stay cooler during the heat.

-You should completely avoid parking in front of a persons' house in a residential area unless you are able to leave really early in the morning. If you want to park in a residential area, park near apartment buildings. This is going to make it easier to blend in. Those in apartments do not own the building and probably won't notice that a new vehicle is there and if they do, they just figure someone is visiting for a few days. On the other hand, those who own their own homes will believe that the curbside that is in front of their home belongs to them, even though it belongs to the city, and they are more likely to call the police in on you.

-If you find that you need to park in a city, it is a good idea to try and park near a university or a college. These are going to have many different vehicles so your van will not stick out as much. In addition, it is sometimes seen as acceptable that a few college students are poor and have to live out of their vehicle so no one is likely to say anything. In addition, lots of the facilities on campuses, including the library, gym showers, and bathrooms are open and available to anyone who needs them. If you are not able to park at a college you can try Walmart parking lots, rest areas, and truck stops as well.

-Always make sure that you are parking in an area that is hidden enough that people are not going to notice that you are staying a lot but out in the open enough that you are not going to get robbed. High crime areas are also places that you must avoid if you do not want to lose your things or get harmed while you are living out of a van. Stealth is also very important because there are many communities who do not want people who are living in vans to be around; think about it, how would you feel if you had children and saw someone getting in and out of a big van? It might seem like it is a little bit creepy and you probably would not want them to stay around. It does not really matter how friendly the person is it is just going to make them nervous and this is why you will encounter a lot of laws that are against people living in vans. It is best to find place to park that are not going to arouse suspicion so that you can live in peace.

There are many different places that you are going to be able to park your van in order to live. The place that you park is often going to depend on the goals that you have in mind along with the area of the country that you live in. For example, if you plan on traveling around and visiting friends and family a lot, the parking spot is not going to be that difficult.

You can stay at some campgrounds or rest stops along the way and then just stay in front of friends' or family members' home and no one is going to bug you. On the other hand, if you are living out of a van in order to save money and you want to find places in your home city that you can stay at, you are going to have to use a little bit more stealth in order to get away with it all. You will have to get creative to find a place that is going to keep you invisible from prying eyes while also keeping you safe from others who might try and harm you in the process.

You are also going to have to consider the location in the country that you are living. Those who are living in the Midwest and the South might find that it is easy to find isolated areas or camping grounds where they are able to get peace and quiet without anyone else bothering them all of the time. On the other hand, if you live in the city, you are not likely to be able to find somewhere out in the wilderness that is going to be available without having to travel hours to get back to work or to your other obligations. You are going to have to use some other methods in order to hide your van in order to get the hiding spot that you want. You can spend some time looking around in order to stay in parking lots, residential areas and other areas where no one is going to notice that you are staying around so that they will leave you alone.

Make sure to take the time to find just the right area that is going to keep you safe and away from prying eyes.

In Cases of Emergencies

If you are living out of your van, it is important to realize that there are emergencies that could occur and you need to be prepared for the worst in case that they do. You would hate to end up in one of these emergencies and not be prepared for what could occur. The first thing that you need to do is make sure that you are prepared for any kind of emergency and that you have some backup plans so that you or anyone else is not going to get hurt.

One of the first things that you will need to do is make sure that you have a cell phone or at least some walkie talkies or radios. You need to have a way that you are able to get in contact with other people in case something is going on. If you get in a crash while you are in your van, you need to be able to get ahold of someone else so that you are not sitting there for hours without the help that you need. If you do not have a way to get the weather or any other alerts, a cell phone can be handy because you can have someone else alert you when these things might be occurring. You should make sure to have a battery that is in good working order and a charger for your phone, especially one that works well in your van without other sources of plugging in so that it can work well when you need it.

Always make sure that your phone is in good working order and that at least a few people have it so that they are able to get ahold of you if something is about to happen. They can alert you if there is a flood that is predicted so that you are not parking in that area or if a tornado is about to hit you can go and find some more secure shelter than your van. There are many reasons that you might need to be contacted so make sure that you have this valuable accessory.

One of the things that you might find will happen when you are in a van are floods. These can cause a lot of damage to your vehicle and you might be stuck drifting off to who knows where if you do not take the right precautions. First, you need to make sure that you have a way to be notified if there is a flood that is coming your way. You might be able to guess that one is likely if you live in an area that floods a lot or in a low valley that could flood with a little bit of rain. You could also keep a radio or some form of weather alert equipment in the van with you to avoid the hassle. This is also where your cell phone might come into use. If there is a flood, it is best to try and stay out of the way. Never park in an area that is low or near the river. Under bridges or in low laying areas are bad ideas as well because it is likely that water is going to collect there and then you and your van are going to be stuck in that area until it is able to recede.

In some cases, you might be stuck going wherever the water is flowing and that could be dangerous as well. It is best to find an area to park that is on higher ground and as far away from the river as possible, especially after a heavy rain or at the end of winter when water melting from up north can cause floods in the south even if there is not any rain.

Flooding is just one of the emergencies that you may be faced with in your time in the van. Another one is tornadoes. This one is of course going to depend on which part of the country you are located in and the time of year. Tornadoes are more likely to occur during the spring and early summer when the two fronts are able to hit each other, although it is possible to get them in the fall as well. Those who live in the Midwest are usually able to tell when the conditions are right for a tornado and just by paying a little bit of attention to the news you should be able to tell when one is likely. This means that for the most part you are going to have some warning that one is about to hit so you can prepare and be ready.

If there is a tornado that is likely to hit your area, it is not a good idea to stay in your van. These are not good places to hide out the strong winds and could actually cause you a lot more damage than good. If the winds get strong enough, they are going to be able to just pick up your van and move you to wherever they want and you will be completely out of control. With the impact of the lift, the drop, and all of the things in your van flying around, you are likely to get hurt and possibly even killed. It is better to find somewhere else that you can stay in the case of a tornado. Find somewhere that you are able to leave your van that is safe a secure as best as you can and just bring along the necessities that would keep you going for a few days if worst comes to worse. You should go and stay with a friend or family member who is in the area if possible. If not, there are often open places in the community that you will be able to go and stay until the bad weather is done. You could check out churches, schools, gyms, or even a grocery store if you are only able to get to that location. Most of the time you will not have an issue finding a place as long as you do not wait too long and the tornado is still a bit away. Never stay with the van. Take care of yourself and deal with the damage later on.

Another emergency that you may come across is a blizzard. This is most prevalent the further up north that you are and hopefully you have had some experience with dealing with this kind of cold and are from the area. For those who are not from the north, the damage that some snow is able to cause does not seem like something that is real and they might not believe that it is that big of a deal. But blizzards are not something that you should mess around with because they are able to cause a lot of damage, make travel almost impossible, and the temperatures around you can drop to dangerous levels within minutes. What starts out with just a few pretty snowflakes can soon leave you stranded and unsafe on the road with nowhere to go for help.

If you have been living out of your van in an area that is known for getting blizzards in the winter, it is best to have another place available where you will be able to go in case a blizzard is about to come. You will have plenty of warning and should know how hard it is going to be in order to keep your van warm once the hard winds hit.

It can also be difficult to find a place to park the van that is going to be out of the way from the wind and which will allow you to get out once the snow is done. If you have some friends or family in the area you might want to consider visiting with them for a few days and staying there if they have some room for you; it is likely that they would be happy to help you out rather than letting you freeze out in the cold. If you are living in an area without any friends or family around, you can go and stop at a motel or see if there is another place in the community that allows others to stay if they need a place. It is just important that you find somewhere that is warm and is going to keep you out of the elements in a way that is much better than what your van is going to be able to do.

There might be times when you get stuck out in a blizzard and you are not able to get to a safe place in time. This could be when you are traveling to the north during winter and did not realize that there was a blizzard that was heading your way. Or you might get into the situation where the blizzard kind of snuck up on you and you did not have any warning.

This can be really dangerous and which is why you should always keep some kind of emergency winter kit in your car so that you are able to stay warm and comfortable if you get stuck.

The first thing that you should do if you get stuck in a blizzard is to pull over and stop. Do not keep driving; this is likely to lead you off the road and you could end up a long way away from where you are going. The further that you drive in the blizzard, the less likely that it will be that you are going to be found. You might end up on a road that is way out in the middle of nowhere or you could end up in a forest or a field and no one will find you once the snow clears up. You also have no idea what you are going to run into along the way so just stop as soon as the blizzard starts since you are not going to be able to see anything that is around in.

Next, if the signal is strong enough you should try to get ahold of someone to let them know where you are. Tell a family member who might be waiting for you on your trip or call the police department and let them know with as much detail where you are located. Tell them the road that you are on as well as a mile marker if you are able to. If you have not been able to keep track of the mile markers or you cannot see them, just give as much information as you are able to such as which towns you are in between or what town you just went through. You probably will not be able to get anyone to help you right away, but if someone knows that you are out there and about where you are located, they will be able to come and help as soon as the roads clear up.

Next, you must make sure that you never leave your vehicle. There have been lots of people who decided that they were better able to get to their destination by foot and then left their van in order to head out. The cold would get to them and they would freeze in the middle of nowhere when they could have been just fine if they stayed in their vehicle and waited for help.

You should always stay in the van no matter what. If you were able to get ahold of someone, they are on their way to help as soon as possible but they will not be able to help if you are out wandering around. Try to keep as warm as possible by keeping the doors and windows shut and bundling up in as many layers and blankets as you can. If you are able to move around the van, do so as much as possible in order to keep warm. You can turn on the van every once in a while to get the heater going to keep warm as well, though try to do this sparingly so that you do not run out of gas. If you have a little grill, use this in order to heat up the area as well. Do whatever you can in order to stay warm, but never leave the vehicle. Someone will be there to help you as soon as they can and your chances of survival are much higher if you stay inside.

Finally, the last big emergency that you may have to face when you are living out of a van is if you get into an accident. This is something that can happen when you are traveling back and forth to different areas, to work, or when you are visiting some friends and family that might be located in different parts of the county. Accidents are something that can happen and can cause a lot of damage and heartache depending on how bad the accident might have been. You could have another car crash into you when you are parked or when driving, slip on some ice or have something else that occurs. It really does not matter what caused the accident, but sometimes the injuries can be severe. If you do end up being in an accident, it is important to get the help that you need right away. You might be harmed, even if you feel fine right at that moment. Call for help and wait for the proper personnel to get there to help out. If you feel like you are really hurt and the accident was more than just a small bump in the back of your van, you should stay put until you can get medical attention. You do not want to get hurt more than you already are or injure something new because you were determine to move around before you got the help that you needed.

Emergencies are a part of life and they are things that you must be prepared for when you are living in a van. You are not going to have all of the personal comforts of home and so you will always need to be on the lookout to get the help and the protection that you need. It is fine to abandon your van if the emergency calls for it; it is likely only going to be for a short little time anyway and then you can go back to the life that you were enjoying when the emergency is over.

Success Stories: Living In A Van

Now that you've learned about minimalist living and in particular, living off the grid in a van, I want you to meet 2 real people who do live in vans and are having the times of their lives. It's my hope that through these people, you'll see that living off the grid in a van is possible.

Bob Wells

He started what is now known as the vandwelling movement back in 1995, during which time he was in the middle of getting a divorce. He bought a box van for just $1,500 and lived there. Despite the very difficult initial transition, he now can't imagine living his life any other way.

After living in a van for the next 6 years, he moved back into a "real" house with a woman he was going out with, thinking he wouldn't have a problem with it. After all, it's the "normal" thing to do. But he was wrong. He couldn't stand normal living in a normal house anymore and because his girl couldn't live in a van, they had to part ways. He moved back into vandwelling.

He never looked back.

Glenn Morrisette

At 46 years old, Glenn is a professional musician and records music for clients in his mobile home and simply emails the finished products to them. Living in an RV and on the road doesn't keep him from living the good life. He has health insurance, eats mostly organic and whole foods and gets to visit places he wants to. Most of all, he's able to do all those things for around $11,000 annually. Yes, you read that right...annually!

In an interview for an article in U.S. News and World Report LP entitled The Secret To Living Well on $11,000 A Year that came out on 20 October 2011, Glenn credited his ability to do so to living fulltime in a van or RV, which according to him, saves him a lot of money because he doesn't have to pay rent and doesn't need a car. Of course, another great reason why he's able to live a full life for just $11,000 a year is because he's a minimalist. He's not big on clothes (he doesn't have to since he works from his mobile home) and rarely eats out because he finds his home cooked healthy meals much more delicious than most restaurants he's eaten in. He confesses to being a frugal person who's not caught up in the consumerist crazy cycle that most people are in.

It Is Possible

Bob and Glenn are just 2 of the many people who have experienced the great joy and excitement of living a minimalist lifestyle off the grid and in a van. Most other people may think that doing so is crazy but as you've seen with these 2 men, it isn't. In fact, it may be that those who are caught up in society's rat race of materialism and dog-eat-dog world may just be the ones who are.

Conclusion

Living in van or other vehicle down isn't the best choice for everyone, but you won't know unless you give it a try! It could be something you plan to do for a few weeks, the summer, or for the long-term.

Everyone has their own ideas about how to be comfortable and the amenities to do so. You will have to take all of that into consideration to see what works for you on a personal level. You can always make modifications to the vehicle if you find that you have outgrown the services that it offers.

Don't be surprised if some of the best memories you have in your life are from this type of experience. It is a great chance to do something unique and even challenging. It can also allow you the opportunity to really appreciate the simple things in life once again.

Too often, many of us get wrapped up in technological devices, fancy clothes, and high dollar cars. Being comfortable, living simple, and having a small amount of overhead and upkeep can help reduce stress and give peace of mind. It will certainly allow you to sleep better at night and enjoy all that you have in your life to be thankful for!

Have fun! Be safe! Step off the grid...

RECOMMENDED READING

Prepping: How To Survive : Natural Disasters, Nuclear Wars and The End Of The World

smarturl.it/preppera

MIND CONTROL: Manipulation, Deception and Persuasion Exposed

hyperurl.co/mindcontrol

Walking: Weight Loss Motivation: Lose Weight, Burn Fat & Increase Metabolism

hyperurl.co/walking

Preppers: Food and Survival Guide: Survival Pantry

hyperurl.co/pantry

Printed in Great Britain
by Amazon